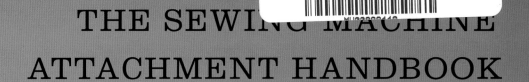

THE SEWING MACHINE ATTACHMENT HANDBOOK

Charlene Phillips

kp

CINCINNATI, OHIO

mycraftivity.com
CONNECT. CREATE. EXPLORE.

The Sewing Machine Attachment Handbook.
Copyright © 2009 by Charlene Phillips.
Manufactured in China. All rights reserved. No
part of this book may be reproduced in any
form or by any electronic or mechanical means
including information storage and retrieval
systems without permission in writing from
the publisher, except by a reviewer who may
quote brief passages in a review. Published by
Krause Publications, an imprint of F+W Media,
Inc., 4700 East Galbraith Road, Cincinnati,
Ohio, 45236. (800) 289-0963. First Edition.

To the best of the Author's knowledge the
work contains no matter which would be
libelous or defamatory, no infringe any
trade name or trademark, or invade any
right of privacy or proprietary right.

Other fine Krause Publications
titles are available from your
local bookstore, craft supply
store, online retailer or visit our
website at www.fwmedia.com.

13   12   11   10   5   4   3

DISTRIBUTED IN CANADA BY FRASER DIRECT
100 Armstrong Avenue
Georgetown, ON, Canada L7G 5S4
Tel: (905) 877-4411

DISTRIBUTED IN THE U.K. AND EUROPE BY
DAVID & CHARLES
Brunel House, Newton Abbot, Devon, TQ12 4PU,
England
Tel: (+44) 1626 323200
Fax: (+44) 1626 323319
Email: postmaster@davidandcharles.co.uk

DISTRIBUTED IN AUSTRALIA BY
CAPRICORN LINK
P.O. Box 704, S. Windsor NSW, 2756 Australia
Tel: (02) 4577-3555

Library of Congress Cataloging in Publication Data
Phillips, Charlene.
  The sewing machine attachment handbook /
Charlene Phillips.
     p. cm.
  Includes index.
  ISBN 978-0-89689-923-0 (pbk. : alk. paper)
  1. Machine sewing--Handbooks, manuals, etc.
  2. Sewing machines--Handbooks, manuals, etc.
  I. Title.
  TT713.P53 2009
  646.2'044--dc22
                                        2008056107

Edited by Stefanie Laufersweiler
Production edited by Julie Hollyday
Designed by Michelle Thompson
Production coordinated by Matthew Wagner
Photography by Tim Grondin and Al Parrish
Illustrations by Hayes Shanesy

ABOUT THE AUTHOR

Charlene Phillips lives in southwestern Ohio with her husband, Bryan. They own and operate The Sew Box, specializing in sewing attachments and books. At The Sew Box, a refurbished sewing machine will be lovingly cleaned and repaired to continue its life of service. More information can be found at www.thesewbox.com. Charlene enjoys sharing tips and hints through her blog at http://thesewbox.blogspot.com and also at www.sewing-attachments.com.

A former public school teacher and college professor, Charlene has always enjoyed instructing others and sharing her expertise. In addition to teaching, Charlene also had a successful seamstress business for over ten years, sewing for others and doing alterations and repairs. Now writing has become another way to share her love for sewing. She has written books on the Singer Featherweight and an assortment of Singer sewing machines and their corresponding attachments. These are presently available only through her Web site.

METRIC CONVERSION CHART

To convert	to	multiply by
Inches	Centimeters	2.54
Centimeters	Inches	0.4
Feet	Centimeters	30.5
Centimeters	Feet	0.03
Yards	Meters	0.9
Meters	Yards	1.1

ACKNOWLEDGMENTS

This book would not have extended farther than my own computer without:

The support of my husband, Bryan, who spends days scouring flea markets and antique malls searching for those odd-looking metal sewing attachments, machines and books;

The lifelong support and encouragement of my mother and father, Virgia and Charles Smith, who urged me to pursue what I enjoy and to always aim high;

The reality checks from my two sons, Troy and Charles, who always ask, "What are those things? Looks like a science experiment!";

The many discussions about the differences in tuckers, rufflers and adjustable zipper feet with my lovely daughter, Shirley, who listened patiently to her mother's ramblings;

The shared love of sewing of my sister Monica Helton, and the interest and frequent ribbing from my brother Mike Smith, who still holds some attachments "hostage" from me;

And Dolores Smith, who provided me with valuable feedback.

If not for these wonderful people, this book would have stayed on my wish list of things to do.

Thank you to all my family, who always gives me that extra push of encouragement. Families are the true treasures in life, and I hold my family treasures dear to my heart!

How do you thank far-reaching sewing friends and fellow sewing fanatics who gave of their time to read, review and give suggestions and honest feedback? A grateful thank-you to Andrea in Washington, Liz and Catherine in Michigan, Rosalind and Linda in California, and Barb in Australia for all their support, encouragement and time. A special thank-you to Clare in California for helping me locate attachments for research. Thank you to the many, many more who requested that this book be written for them.

Books such as this would not be possible without the assistance and support of many who are not only experts in their craft, but dedicated to providing the best book possible to you, the reader. A special thank-you to editor Stefanie Laufersweiler, who immediately put me at ease, guided the process flawlessly and kept me on track. Many thanks to design director Michelle Thompson for her design capabilities; it is truly a gift to be able to have a vision of how a book should flow. Thank you also to photographer Tim Grondin, who is a master in his craft, and to associate editor Julie Hollyday, who smilingly jumped in to help. There are very special people at KP Craft Books and all were coordinated by managing editor Vanessa Lyman.

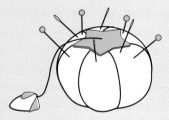

DEDICATION

For my family of the past and the present—including my grandchildren, Chance, Corin and Maggie—and those still unborn, who are the future.

Contents

INTRODUCTION—*6*

A BRIEF HISTORY OF ATTACHMENTS—*8*

TYPES OF SEWING MACHINES—*12*

WHAT TO LOOK FOR IN A SEWING MACHINE—*15*

SETTING UP YOUR MACHINE—*19*
Solving Some Common Problems—22

DETERMINING YOUR SHANK TYPE—*23*

CLAMPING ATTACHMENTS ONTO YOUR MACHINE—*24*

Using Your Attachments—*26*

Attachment Foot—28

Cloth Guide (Seam Guide)—32

Bias Cutting Gauge—36

Binder—40

Bias-Tape Maker and Fusible-Tape Maker—44

Adjustable Tape-Stitching Presser Foot—48

Tucker—52

Ruffler—56

Foot Hemmer—62

Hemmer Set—66

Adjustable Hemmer—70

Edge Stitcher—74

Gathering Foot—78

Double Shirring Foot—82

Adjustable Zipper/ Cording Foot—86

Welting Foot—90

Felling Foot—94

Darning/Embroidery/ Free-Motion Quilting Foot—98

Quilting Foot—102

Walking Foot—106

Sequin Foot—110

Buttonholer—114

Braiding Presser Foot—120

Underbraider—124

Stitch-in-the-Ditch Foot—128

Stocking Darner—132

Zigzagger—136

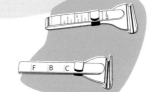

RESOURCES—*141*

INDEX—*142*

Introduction

WHY THE INTEREST in vintage sewing machine attachments, especially when today we have computerized sewing machines doing everything at the push of a button? For me, it all started with one sewing machine and those metal oddities I discovered in the bottom of the case.

My interest began when my mother taught me to sew. We started with doll clothes, then aprons, pinafores and, finally, school clothes. Hours were spent cutting and sewing. I also remember my grandmother creating beautiful items. Although her interest was crocheting, she was still creating something to treasure from a piece of cloth or skein of yarn. After learning the basics, we each moved on to new challenges. For me, it was learning how to use those wonderful metal oddities that are sewing machine attachments and tools.

After some research, I began using those oddities to turn out hemmed and ruffled garments, bound buttonholes, aprons embellished with braids, laces and flounces, and pillows decorated with dainty tucking. If you're like me, soon you'll begin thinking of the next attachment to acquire. Before long, my sewing friend, you'll be scouring yard sales and flea markets for a new metal oddity.

As your eyes begin to blaze with excitement, take a deep breath and realize everything is fine. You have merely caught on to the obsessive nature of owning these wonderfully complex-looking attachments, which are simple to use, once you learn the basics.

Using your attachments will add a personal touch to your sewing projects. You might remember when your mother or grandmother sewed her family's clothes on a treadle sewing machine. With the continual invention of new sewing machine attachments, methods quickly changed. Instead of painstakingly hand-sewing each tuck on the front of a child's blouse, you could complete the task more quickly with a tucker. Making rows and rows of ruffles became a breeze using the ruffler. When money was tight, a darning attachment mended clothes; when money was more plentiful, an embroidery attachment created treasures for the home. Early sewing machines were designed for straight stitching only. Sewing attachments were designed to replicate more complicated hand stitching, making the task of sewing more enjoyable.

With this book, you will learn to use your sewing attachments to form tucks, make bound buttonholes, add lace or even create your own lace. What better compliment to hear than, "Wow! That is gorgeous! You made that?" You will discover the joy of using your attachments as you quickly master each one. These tools will provide endless hours of enjoyment and satisfaction. Just relax and have fun!

A Brief History of Attachments

The invention of new sewing machine attachments through the years closely followed fashion. Details that were accomplished first through hand sewing soon were done with a "modern-day invention." As fashions began showing embellishments of soutache braid, the braiding attachment was invented. Over the years, more attachments were invented to replicate fine detailing by hand. In 1873, F. W. Brown of Cincinnati, Ohio, patented an "Improvement to Tuckers for Sewing Machines." The patent list continues with contributions by other inventors— some well known, some more obscure—who each made the art of sewing a little easier.

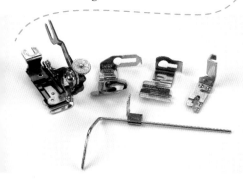

The Griest Manufacturing Company, advertised as "Manufacturers of the World's Finest Sewing Machine Attachments...Metal Stamping....Assembly Specialists since 1870."

Griest/Greist Manufacturing Company

In 1879, the Griest Manufacturing Company began selling sewing machines. Flash forward seventy-six years to the publication of an instructional booklet explaining the use of sewing machine attachments made by the *Greist* Manufacturing Company. Despite the spelling difference, one man was responsible for both: John M. Griest (1850–1906).

One of Griest's earliest patents was an improved hemmer in 1873. Over the next sixteen years, he received more than twenty-one patents for various sewing machine inventions, including several assigned to the Chicago Attachment Company and to the Singer Manufacturing Company. Some of his inventions included the ruffler, gatherer, buttonholer, tuck-marker, braiding foot and sewing guide.

In 1879, he formed the Griest Manufacturing Company and began making a sewing machine advertised as an "Improved Singer," marketed as better than that produced by Singer. Each Griest machine was furnished with a foot hemmer, feller, braider, twelve needles, six bobbins, screwdriver, oil can with oil, extra check spring, extra throat plate, gauge, gauge screw, wrench, quilter and instruction book. You could purchase the No. 1 machine in a plain table for fifteen dollars or the No. 12 machine with full cabinet and fancy folding cover for forty dollars.

In 1881, Griest returned to developing sewing machine attachments, and again his inventions were assigned to and carried the name of the Singer Manufacturing Company for the next eleven years. One of his last inventions for Singer, registered in 1889, was the "Patented Folding Box" for attachment styles 1, 3, 7, 8, 9 and 11. Collectors today know it as the "puzzle box."

In 1892, with the spelling of his last name changed, John M. Greist founded the Greist Manufacturing Company, "manufacturer of sewing machine attachments and bicycle supplier." His inventions and production of sewing machine attachments continued until his death around 1906, and was carried on by at least two more generations. Today we attribute many of our present-day sewing machine attachments to the ingenuity of John M. Greist.

Western Electric and Graybar Manufacturing Companies

Elisha Gray and Enos Barton began their partnership in 1869, founding Gray & Barton in Ohio. The original company produced burglar alarms and answer-back call boxes. Its name was changed to Western Electric Company in 1872. During the first two decades of the twentieth century, Western Electric was one of the largest distributors of electrical equipment in the United States.

By 1926, Western Electric had become so large that a separate entity for handling distribution of supplies and equipment was established. The new entity was named Graybar, after the original founders Gray and Barton. Graybar was the largest merchandiser of electrical supplies in the world. In the 1930s, Graybar, under the Graybar brand name, merchandised appliances such as electric fans, toy ranges and sewing machines. During the company's history, it distributed machines such as the Western Electric No. 1 Portable and the Graybar No. 2 Rotary.

Attachments for sewing machines were becoming increasingly popular. What was once done by hand was now achieved with a sewing machine attachment. Attachments supplied with the Western Electric No. 1 Vibrator machine were the binder, hemmer set, braider foot, ruffler, underbraider, tucker and screwdrivers. Attachments for the No. 2 Rotary machine were the binder, hemmer set, shirrer, braider foot, ruffler, underbraider, bias cutting gauge, tucker, edge stitcher and screwdrivers.

An instruction manual from the early 1920s devotes one full page to "needles for Western Electric No. 1 Portable Sewing Machines." It lists over 270 sewing companies, including Excelsior, Famous, Goodrich, Happy Home, Minneapolis, Oxford, Pan-American, Rival, Ruby, Singer, Strange, Triumph and World's Fair. Listed on the page were many of the earlier sewing machine companies.

Graybar later produced a manual explaining how to use sewing machine attachments. The instructions applied mainly to the No. 1 Vibrator, No. 2 Rotary, No. 4 Two Spool, Nos. 5 and 6 Console, and the No. 7 Cabinet sewing machines.

Although Western Electric and Graybar Electric Company are noted mostly for electrical equipment, their contributions to the history of household sewing are important.

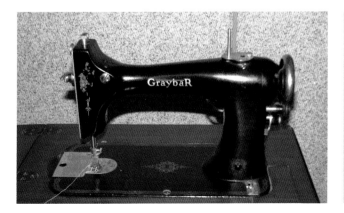

During the 1930s, Graybar marketed its own brand of appliances and sewing machines. (photo courtesy of Graybar)

Willcox & Gibbs

The Willcox & Gibbs Sewing Machine Company was founded in 1859, with multiple branches eventually established in the United States, London, Paris, Milan and Brussels.

James Edward Allen Gibbs, a farmer from Virginia, patented his first chain-stitch single-thread sewing machine in 1857, patent number 17,427. The machine has patents listed on its machine plate dating from 1857 to 1861, under the names of J. E. A. Gibbs, James and Charles Willcox & Carleton, and Charles H. Willcox. Each date correlates to patented improvements.

In 1857, Willcox & Gibbs advertised its chain-stitch machine as "the noiseless automatic." You could finish your mending without disturbing others. If you look at the back of a Willcox & Gibbs sewing machine, the shape of the machine head is a perfect G, a clever way to always recognize the machine invented by Gibbs.

Attachments made by Willcox & Gibbs were specifically made for their machines only. Each attachment was designed to fit into a precise niche formed in the cast of the machine. The ruffler, for example, has hooks which must fit specifically within a hole in the sewing machine. Likewise, the quilter must be placed in a certain spot. Certainly, much forethought was given during the production of each machine and the invention of attachments. Needless

Willcox & Gibbs advertised their newly patented machine as "the noiseless automatic."

to say, only attachments produced by Willcox & Gibbs could be used with their treadle and hand-crank sewing machines.

Attachments for the Willcox & Gibbs machines included an improved tucker, a wrench for inserting the needle, a quilter, a cloth guide and nut, a linen and flannel hemmer, a wide hemmer and feller, a narrow hemmer, various hemmer nuts and a gatherer.

The original cost for a Willcox & Gibbs Improved Tucker was two dollars. This attachment allowed you to make narrow or wide tucks. An advertisement for hemmers lists No. 1 to No. 18, all designed for a special style of sewing, from wide hems to the insertion of lace on top.

Singer Sewing Machine Company

The Singer Sewing Machine Company was another leading producer of sewing machine attachments. Isaac M. Singer, in partnership with Edward Clark, formed I. M. Singer & Company in June 1851. They first produced industrial sewing machines, such as the Vibrating Shuttle No. 1 and the No. 2 Standard. In 1856, they manufactured their first sewing machine aimed at the domestic household.

Also in 1856, Singer's company patented a ruffler, a tucker and a binder to meet the growing desire to add decorative touches to home sewing. Singer began including basic attachment sets with each sewing machine; special attachments such as the tucker were sold separately.

Singer categorized its sewing attachments, referring to them as regular attachments, fashion aids and special attachments. The regular attachments were included with most sewing machines and included the binder, edge stitcher, gatherer, hemmer, adjustable hemmer and ruffler. Fashion aids included items such as the blind stitch braider, corder foot, darning and embroidery attachment, and walking presser foot, to name a few. The last category included those most expensive items at the time and those rarely seen today, such as the two-thread embroidery attachment, tubular trimmer and the underbraider.

The Singer Sewing Machine Company opened its first Singer Sewing Center in New York City in 1927 to teach others how to use Singer sewing machines and attachments. By 1951, Singer had trained over 400,000. Singer was the first to develop the "installment plan" for purchases. For as little as five dollars down and monthly payments around three dollars, you could rent or lease the machine until it was paid for.

Over the years the Singer name changed four times, yet the Singer quality and trademark remained.

* 1851 – I. M. Singer & Company
* 1853 – Singer Manufacturing Company
* 1904 – Singer Sewing Machine Company
* 1963 – The Singer Company

Today, Singer continues the tradition began by Isaac M. Singer, selling sewing machines and attachments the world over.

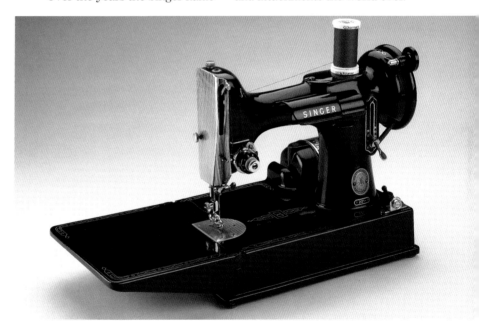

In 1933, Singer introduced its new Featherweight sewing machine at the Chicago World's Fair.

Types of Sewing Machines

In the past century alone, close to 46,000 sewing machine patents of various types have been issued. The smallest sewing machine, a toy, weighs around 3 pounds (1.4kg); the largest industrial machine weighs 900 pounds (408kg).

Of course, you probably are not looking for a child's machine or an industrial one; you want a sewing machine that does straight stitching, decorative stitching, embroidery and possibly quilting. What might you find at flea markets, yard sales or on the Internet?

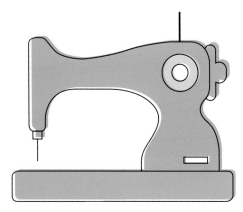

A mechanical sewing machine requires you to manipulate the controls by hand.

Mechanical Machines

From the mid-1800s until about the late 1960s, all sewing machines were mechanical. Early machines used a bullet-shaped shuttle bobbin case and a back-and-forth oscillating hook, while newer mechanical machines had a rotating hook. Most basic mechanical machines sew a straight stitch only, while others might offer zigzagging for decorative stitching.

A mechanical sewing machine is controlled by a rotary wheel. Adjustments for such things as tension and stitch length are controlled by moving a dial. There are basically three categories: straight stitch, semiautomatic and automatic.

Straight-stitch machines go forward and backward, and allow stitch regulation. Some may have the capacity to lower the feed dogs for darning and embroidery.

Semiautomatic zigzag machines have all the features of the straight-stitch machines, plus the zigzag stitch and the ability to create buttonholes, sew stretchy fabrics and do blind hemming.

Automatic zigzag machines provide straight stitching, zigzag stitching, stretch stitching, buttonholes and blind hems. In addition, they usually come with a variety of decorative stitches built in. Some offer additional decorative stitches through special cams you purchase separately.

Electronic Machines

During the 1970s, electronic sewing machines became popular, having all the features of the mechanical machines and more—at the push of a button. Electronic models rely on computerized chips to do some of the tedious jobs for you. The machines offer a wealth of stitches with touchpad controls and, on some models, an LED screen. Stitch widths, lengths and optimum tensions are built into the machine, yet you can still adjust them manually if you wish.

FUN FACT

A household machine can stitch about 1,500 to 2,000 stitches per minute, yet it can be stopped in a second.

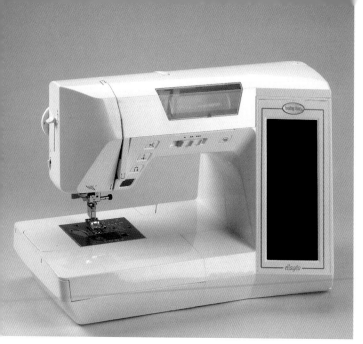

Computer programs for different stitches are stored on a removable cartridge or memory disk. Some can be hooked directly to a PC to download patterns.

Computerized Machines

As sewing machines became more complex, more motors were added, with a computer coordinating the functions. Repetitive sequences of stitches are programmed into the machine; you no longer have to replicate these movements time and time again.

The computerized sewing machine is similar to the electronic sewing machines in that it uses the same basic chips and motors as the electronic, but it also has a microprocessor. This allows the machine to accept new information, usually from an insertable card, and then create patterns from the instructions loaded on that specific card. This is similar to loading a software program onto your computer. When you add new programs, the computer simply reads them; likewise, a computerized sewing machine will read any different patterns you add.

All computerized sewing machines can work like a mechanical or be set to sew the designs generated by the program on the card. You decide the pattern and where to place it; the rest is automatic. Embroidery machines fall into this category.

Sergers

The serger's function is to cut and finish the edge of the material, providing a finished seam just as in commercially produced clothing. A serger uses loopers to make the stitch, similar to knitting needles. A set of upper and lower knives cuts the material just before it is sewn, similar to a pair of scissors in action.

Although a serger can be an aid to your sewing, you will still need to have a sewing machine for straight stitching. You can certainly sew a pair of pants very quickly with a serger; however, you will need a straight-stitch machine to finish the hem or reinforce stress areas. You can sew a blouse quite nicely with a serger, but you'll need your sewing machine for darts or decorative finishes.

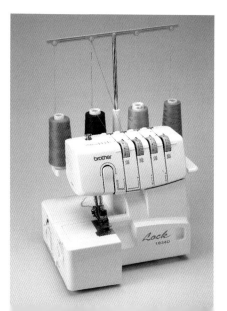

A serger trims and finishes seams, producing a professional finish. Planning your sewing project before you begin stitching will allow you to utilize your serger as much as possible in the construction.

What to Look for in a Sewing Machine

Buying a used sewing machine can be overwhelming because so many choices are available. Are you interested in straight-stitch or zigzag, a portable or cabinet model, open arm or flat bed, mechanical or electronic?

Begin by assessing your needs and sewing skills. If you're a beginner, think about how your needs may change as your skills improve. Will you take sewing classes? If so, consider the weight of the machine and the ease of transporting it. You'll also want to avoid any mechanical problems. There are many factors to consider besides the machine itself, so let's start with the basics.

* **Your Sewing Projects**
  Do you plan to make clothes for you and your family?
  Will you make household and decorative items?
  Do you quilt?
  Will you make draperies, slipcovers or bedspreads?
     Will you use it for mending and simple alterations?

* **Durability**
  Do you plan to use the machine for several months? Several years? A lifetime?

* **Size and Location**
  What room will you sew in? Will the machine stay up or will you store it between projects?
  Will you store it in the closet? An extra room?
  Do you want a cabinet?
  Do you want a portable? Is the case included or available to buy?

* **Cost**
  How much machine can you afford?
  How much do the features and accessories you want cost?

Do Your Homework

The Internet can provide you with a wealth of information on what's available. Create a list of what features you are looking for. Remember that each new feature will require additional knowledge and practice if you want to make full use of your machine. List some possibile machines and compare features and costs.

Talk to dealers at a nearby sewing center about used models. Test each machine, and then go home and think about what you really need. This is when you might begin to feel dizzy and overwhelmed with so many choices. Never allow yourself to be pushed into a newer model with all the state-of-the art features; it may not be the best buy for you.

Talk to friends and experienced sewers about their successes and frustrations. What do they wish they could have or what could they live without?

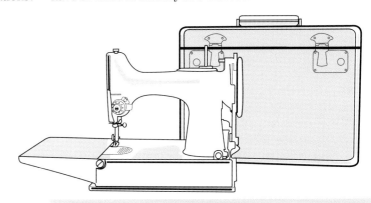

A case for your portable sewing machine is a wise investment. You can easily carry it to sewing class and keep it dust free.

What Features Do You Need?

A machine with an automatic needle threader may be tempting; however, there are many inexpensive stand-alone needle threaders you can purchase.

Your bobbin choices include top-loading or side-loading. Top-loading machines let you insert the bobbin from the top, while side-loading bobbins are inserted under the needle plate. Once you use the bobbin several times, you'll have no problem with either.

A feed-dog adjustment lowers the feed dogs for embroidery, darning or freehand quilting. If you find a used sewing machine without this capability, you're still fine; you'll just need to use a darning/embroidery plate. These are readily available for most machines, either as originals or reproductions.

A removable flat bed will allow you to stitch around small openings such as sleeves.

When Shopping

Weigh the cost factor against what you will truly use during regular sewing, your present sewing ability, and future progress. If you're purchasing a used machine from a dealer, ask about a cabinet or carrying case, added accessories and attachments, and classes. If there is a warranty, ask what it covers and for how long.

Test each machine that you are interested in. No matter who is selling it, ask to plug it in and test all the functions. As you shop, take along swatches of fabric, thread and extra needles. Sew forward and in reverse; test the stitch and tension regulators and the knee control; use all of the stitches available.

If an extra bobbin is available, it is a good idea to wind a bobbin to ensure the bobbin winding unit works properly.

Testing the machine can make the difference between buying one that will give you hours of pleasurable sewing, or buying a frustrating machine that you will ultimately stick in the closet.

Seeking a Mechanically Sound Machine

It isn't difficult to find a mechanically sound machine, and that is your primary goal. Many people trade up to newer models, leaving you the opportunity to buy a used but fully functional sewing machine at an affordable price.

Has the machine been well cared for? Ask the seller how long they have had it and if they bought it new. What does it look like cosmetically? This can be a strong indication of care and proper maintenance. There are many older machines that have had very little use; however, some may have been used in a factory setting.

Does the machine sound smooth and quiet while running? Does it sew at a good speed? If you feel like you are pressing on the foot control as hard as you can and the machine still pokes along, or if the motor sounds unusually loud or vibrates excessively, then there is a good chance some major repairs might be required. Many people enjoy the task of finding wonderful vintage machines and refurbishing them into almost new condition. If you are not one of these, continue shopping.

Check for scratches or dents. Normal scratching comes from years of use. Deep scratches and gouges may catch your material as you sew.

Be sure the bobbin case is intact. Most replacements are inexpensive; however, some models could add another fifty dollars to your actual cost. Check the bobbin case and the bobbin for burrs. These can prevent your thread from forming the proper stitch and cause thread breakage. Remove the bobbin and rub inside the bobbin case with your finger, checking for anything that "grabs" you.

Check for missing parts. As you sew, adjust the tension to ensure no parts are missing from the tension knob. The same goes for the bobbin winding unit. Are the needle plates on the machine and do they fit properly? Does it have a regular presser foot attached?

If there are belts, are they on the machine? Check any visible belts for heavily worn spots. If everything else looks great but the machine's lacking a belt, no problem. Belts are inexpensive and available at most fabric stores or repair shops.

Is the foot control or knee lever easy to operate? If you are pressing on either and not going anywhere fast, the they might need repaired or replaced.

Finally, check the electrical cord and plug for damage.

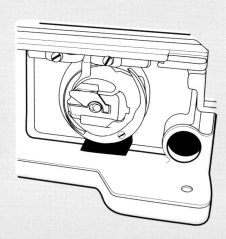

Depending on the model, bobbins may be inserted from the side by lifting the machine bed, or they may be top-loaded.

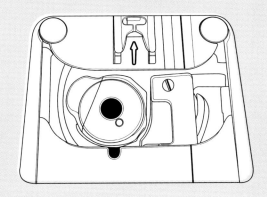

Beyond Mechanics

Is an instruction manual included? If not, but the machine is in good condition and worth the price, many companies carry replacement manuals.

Are attachments included? If not, can they be readily purchased?

Do you have a local sewing machine repair shop, or are you able to perform the normal maintenance procedures, such as replacing belts, oiling and making simple adjustments?

Lastly, don't be fooled by take-your-breath-away beauty. A sturdy machine might be underneath, but keep in mind that what you really want is a machine that will sew, is easy to use, and can be repaired if necessary.

Troubleshooting While Shopping

Sometimes a simple adjustment is all that's necessary to solve some common problems.

* **Top thread breaking.**
  Try a different thread.
  Rethread.
  See if the thread is caught on the spool.
  Ensure the needle is inserted correctly.
      Check for a bent needle.
  Loosen the top tension.
  Inspect the bobbin hook for burrs;
      polish it with a fine emery cloth.

* **Loops on the bottom.**
  Tighten the top tension.
  Check for something caught in the tension
      spring. Use a thin card to clear.
  Rethread.
  Open the bobbin case to see if the bobbin
      fits snugly inside it. If the size is incorrect,
      replacement bobbins are very inexpensive.

* **Loose thread on the top.**
  Adjust the top tension; turn clockwise.

* **Skipped stitches.**
  Replace the needle, inserting it as far as it will go.
  Loosen the pressure regulator.

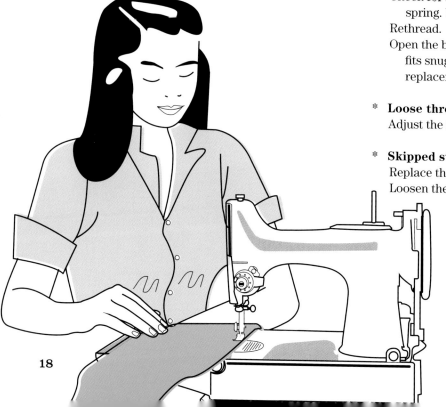

18

Setting Up Your Machine

Why isn't my attachment working correctly? Is it defective in some way? As you go from straight stitching to using any new attachment, always practice first on scrap material to ensure your tension, stitch length and pressure are correct. Anytime you make a change, whether adding an attachment, using different fabric or thread, or even using a new needle, your sewing machine may require some slight adjustment in one or all three areas.

Stitch Length Regulator

All sewing machines have a stitch length regulator that allows you to change your stitch length. The numbers on your stitch regulator may be based on the inch or metric system of measurement.

Stitch length may be controlled by either a lever or a knob. To change the length of your stitch using a lever, screw the thumb nut away from the stitch indicator plate as far as it will go. Then move the stitch regulator until it is in line with the number indicating your desired stitch length. Tighten the thumb nut inward until it touches the stitch indicator plate. If your machine is controlled by a knob, turn it either left or right to the desired number.

TIP

Use a shorter stitch when sewing on the bias or curved seams to increase the elasticity of the seam.

STITCH LENGTH REGULATOR
Use the stitch length regulator for backstitching—sewing in reverse and forward over the same stitches to lock the seam.

Common Stitch Lengths

* **5–6 stitches per inch (or 4 to 5mm stitches):** Long stitches are used for basting and topstitching.

* **10–12 stitches per inch (or 2.5 to 3mm stitches):** This is the average stitch length for medium-weight fabrics.

* **13–20 stitches per inch (or 2mm stitches):** Short stitches are used for lightweight fabrics, as well as for satin stitching and other decorative effects.

PRESSURE REGULATOR
Many sewing machines today have an automatic pressure regulator, whereas older models may have the screw type.

Pressure Regulator

Proper stitching requires the correct amount of pressure on your fabric to ensure even feeding of the layers. The correct amount of pressure will depend on the weight of the fabric. Medium-weight material will require an intermediate pressure. When sewing thin or silky fabrics, you will need to reduce the pressure of the machine. When sewing heavier fabrics, increase the pressure.

It may be difficult to achieve the correct pressure to evenly feed materials such as leather, vinyl, velvet, fur and other pile fabrics. In these cases, use an accessory such as the even feed or walking foot to achieve an even stitch.

As you adjust the pressure regulator, remember that you want enough pressure to prevent creeping of the material while maintaining that beautiful stitch. The amount of force the presser foot places on your fabric is normally controlled by a pressure regulator located either on the machine arm or on top of the machine. Some newer machines have an automatic pressure adjustment mechanism that doesn't require any manual adjustment. Depending on the type of regulator on your sewing machine, adjustments may be made in several ways.

* **Dial on the side or on the top.** Marked with either words or numerals. Words are self-explanatory; with numerals, the higher the number, the greater the pressure.

* **Push bar.** A push bar regulator has a lock-release collar around it. When the bar is pushed down to increase the pressure, the collar locks into place. When the collar is pushed, the bar is released and pressure is decreased.

* **Screw type.** Turn clockwise to increase the pressure, counterclockwise to decrease it.

Tension Control

Every sewing machine has a tension control for the top thread, and most have one for the bobbin thread. The tension controls increase or decrease the pressure on the threads as they move through the sewing machine, determining how much thread is fed into each stitch. Even stitches are achieved as the top and the bottom threads are "locked" in the center.

Too much tension will result in too little thread for the stitch. Too little thread causes puckering and strained stitches. Not enough tension results in too much thread being fed through the machine, which causes weak, loopy stitches.

Always test the tension when beginning a new project or when adding any attachments to your sewing machine. A simple change of fabric, thread, needle or attachment can affect how the thread feeds through your sewing machine. For your test, use the same type of fabric, the same number of fabric layers, and the same thread and needle you will be using for your project, and then make the necessary adjustments.

If the stitches are too tight, decrease the tension by turning the control knob to the left. Lower numbers indicate less tension. If your stitches are too loose, increase the tension by turning the knob to the right. Higher numbers indicate increased tension. Normally, fine threads require a lower tension, while heavy cotton or linen thread requires more tension to produce the perfect stitch.

TENSION CONTROL
Setting no. 4 is a good place to begin when adjusting your tension.

Solving Some Common Problems

Looped stitching underneath the fabric may be caused by an incorrect tension. Loops on the top may indicate improper threading.

* **Pressure regulator is hard to adjust.**

  The presser foot may not have been lowered before you tried to adjust the pressure.

  The pressure regulator may be turned to the maximum setting. Try turning it the other way. If this does not make a difference, the regulator may need to be serviced.

* **Layers feed unevenly.**

  The pressure may be too heavy or too light.

  Try stitching more slowly.

  When sewing slippery or very lightweight fabrics, you might try using either tissue paper or thin pellon underneath the fabric while stitching.

  You may need to use an attachment that will help feed the fabric evenly.

* **Fabric puckers when stitched.**

  Most fabrics will pucker when stitched in a single layer.

  If the fabric is lightweight or sheer, the stitch length should not be too long and the pressure regulator should be loosened.

  If the fabric is knitted or tightly woven, the stitch length may be too short.

  Stitch tension may be unbalanced. Adjust the tension control.

Puckered stitching may be caused by an unbalanced tension. Try moving to a larger number.

* **Stitches have loops between them.**

  If the loops are large, your machine may be improperly threaded. Loops on the bottom of the fabric indicate the thread is not securely seated between the tension discs. Loops on the top of the fabric indicate the thread is not properly inserted into the bobbin case.

  If the loops are smaller, the tension is probably unbalanced. If the loops are on the bottom, tighten the upper tension; if the loops are on the top, loosen the upper tension.

  There might not be enough pressure to hold the fabric taut during sewing. Adjust your pressure regulator.

* **Stitches are uneven lengths.**

  You just might be pulling or pushing the fabric too much. Let the machine do the work; just guide it.

  The pressure on the presser foot could be too heavy or too light for the fabric. Try adjusting the pressure regulator.

* **Stitches skip here and there.**

  You might have the wrong size needle for the fabric.

  The needle might be bent.

  Check to see if the needle is inserted correctly for your machine (it might be inserted backwards).

  There might not be enough pressure on the presser foot. Adjust the pressure regulator.

Determining Your Shank Type

One of the first dilemmas you may face is determining whether your sewing machine uses low, high, slant or snap-on sewing attachments. Most sewing machines produced after 1980 use snap-on feet; however, they may also have the capability of using other shank attachments. If the snap-on ankle can be removed by loosening a thumbscrew, you can also use either the low or slant shank. Determine your shank size by measuring.

* **Low Shank:** measures ½" (13mm)

* **High Shank:** measures 1" (25mm)

* **Slant Shank:** measures about 1" (25mm) and is designed for Singer slant-needle machines

MEASURE YOUR SHANK
Place the presser foot down. Measure from the bed of the machine to the center of the thumbscrew.

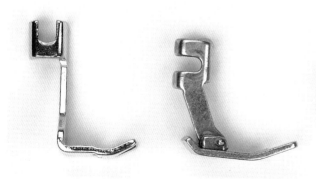

| high shank | slant shank | low shank | snap-on |

Clamping Attachments Onto Your Machine

There were hundreds of sewing machine companies in existence during the late 1800s, and many had their own methods for placing attachments on the presser bar. Not only could each company have a different method, but differences could be found within a company. It is important to determine which type of attachment your machine uses (side-clamp, back-clamp, top-clamp or bed-clamp), especially before purchasing additional attachments.

The sewing machines mentioned for each attachment design below certainly do not constitute an all-inclusive list. With so many types of used sewing machines available for purchase, you will need to carefully note how your presser foot attaches to your particular machine.

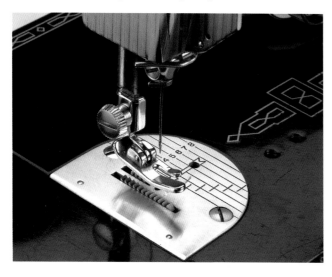

Side-Clamp

Many models of the past and present use a straight, low-shank presser foot, also referred to as side-clamping. A thumbscrew on the side holds the presser foot and attachments in place. Many Singer, Necchi, Brother, Pfaff and early treadles used this design. Today's newer models have evolved into low-shank snap-on designs.

Back-Clamp

The Singer 66-1 is in a class almost alone: it uses a back-clamping foot. A thumbscrew on the back of the presser bar holds the attachments in place. Only one other sewing machine company, Wheeler & Wilson, utilized the back-clamping design.

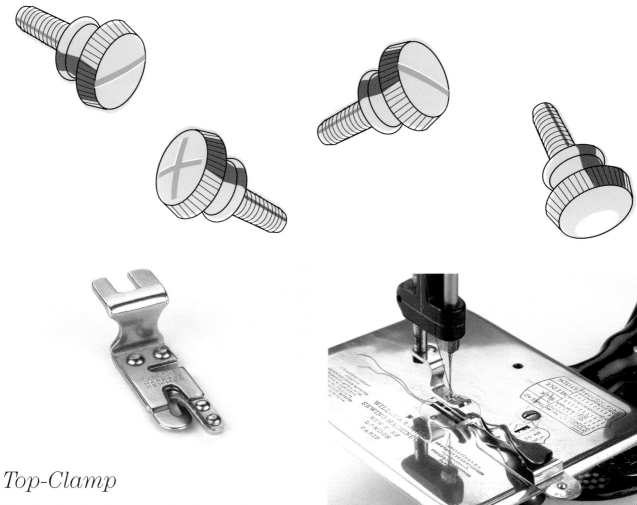

Top-Clamp

Top-clamping attachments are found on machines made by Davis, New Home, Standard, White, Domestic, Kenmore, Free-Westinghouse and National. If your attachments are top-clamping, you will need to determine the size of the slot where it wraps around the presser bar. According to a locating chart distributed by the Boye Needle Company in 1909, there were twelve different widths of slots and styles of shank formation. A chart was necessary to identify which size top-clamping attachment was needed.

Bed-Clamp

Bed-clamping attachments are found on very early transverse shuttle sewing machines such as the Willcox & Gibbs. The attachments are attached to a hole in the machine bed, not on the presser bar.

Using Your Attachments

You have purchased your used sewing machine, brought it home and unpacked it. Now you are ready to sew. There might be some strange and complex-looking sewing attachments hiding in the bottom of the sewing case or in one of the cabinet drawers. Your next step is to learn what each one can do for you, because each one works in a special way.

Some of the attachments on the pages that follow are specific to a single sewing machine company; some were produced by many manufacturers. You may have some of them or all. You might see one that piques your interest and proceed to look for it. Regardless of your sewing machine brand, the attachments and special feet may attach to your machine differently than they do in these illustrations, but they can produce the same results and add that personal touch to your sewing.

The attachment foot was specifically made to attach hemmers of varying sizes directly onto the foot.

A quick-release spring allows a change from one hemmer size to another without removing the attachment foot from your machine. Only with the use of the specially made attachment foot can you use the hemmer set and binder manufactured by Greist. It is essential to have the correct shank for your specific sewing machine. Once you determine whether your machine uses low, slant or high shank attachments, you should find an attachment foot to fit your specific sewing machine.

Using the Attachment Foot

- -

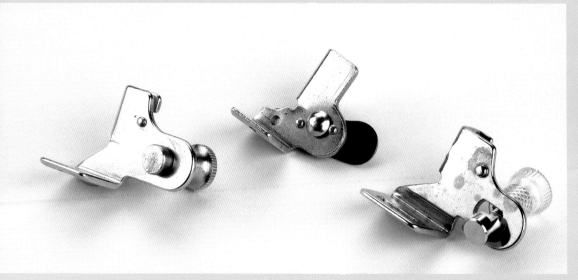

VARIETY OF TYPES AND SIZES OF ATTACHMENT FEET
Over the years, the attachment foot has been produced with a blue release spring and with a thumbscrew.

ATTACHMENT FOOT AND HEMMER
Before using your hemmer or binder, you will need to attach it to the attachment foot. Note the blue spring in the back of the attachment foot and how it correlates to the slot on the hemmer.

LOOKING BACK
In 1892, John M. Greist invented an "attachment holder" for the purpose of placing hemmers of varying sizes directly onto the special foot.

PLACING THE ATTACHMENT FOOT ON THE HEMMER

Press forward on the blue spring and slide the rivet through the hole. Continue sliding the attachment foot to the left until it is in place. Release pressure on the blue spring.

IF YOU HAVE A THUMBSCREW INSTEAD OF A BLUE SPRING

Instead of a blue spring, your attachment foot may have a thumbscrew on the back side. To place the foot onto the hemmer, loosen the screw on the back of the foot. Press the screw forward against the back of the attachment foot to create a space. With the screw pressed forward, slip the large slot in your hemmer or binder onto the screw. Move the attachment foot as far to the left as possible and tighten the screw.

ATTACHING THE ATTACHMENT FOOT TO YOUR MACHINE

Remove your regular presser foot and place the attachment foot onto your machine. Depending upon where you need your stitching, you may need to adjust the attachment to either stitch close to an edge or away from it. Press in on your blue spring (or loosen the screw and press in), slide the hemmer or binder to the left or right as needed, and release the spring (or tighten the screw). Always check to ensure your needle enters the hole and the stitching line falls where needed.

CLOTH GUIDE (Seam Guide)

The cloth guide, often called a seam guide, is designed to ensure straight and accurate seams.

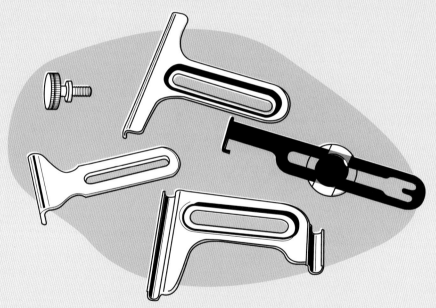

Whether you are piecing a quilt top or adding decorative top-stitching to pockets, you can adjust your seam allowance accordingly. Keeping your eye on the seam guide instead of the needle and keeping your material against the guide will ensure accurate and consistent seam allowances.

Using the Cloth Guide

VARIETY OF TYPES AND SIZES OF CLOTH GUIDES

Cloth guides come in a variety of shapes and sizes. Most are attached to your machine bed using a thumbscrew. You may have an original or a reproduction on your machine.

* With an adjustable cloth guide, you can adjust from a scant quilting seam to more than an inch (25mm) seam allowance without removing the guide. Loosen the thumbscrew and move the guide accordingly. The adjustable cloth guide is designed to also move diagonally, helping you sew accurate curves. Turn it lengthwise when sewing longer seams.

* Another cloth guide you may have in your attachment case has a plastic piece on the bottom, which keeps your machine from becoming scratched. Loosen the thumbscrew and adjust right or left for your seam allowance.

* A magnetic cloth guide is universal to any sewing machine because you can attach it to your machine wherever you need it. To adjust, simply lift it up and place it according to your desired seam width.

ATTACHING THE CLOTH GUIDE TO YOUR MACHINE

The cloth guide is attached to the sewing machine using a thumbscrew. Place the guide over the holes to the right of the needle. Insert the screw into the proper hole on your sewing machine bed. Using the screw, attach the guide to your machine. Most sewing machines will have two holes to the right of the needle. Which hole you insert the screw into depends upon your machine. The hole on the left may have mechanics of your sewing machine underneath, while the right may not, or vice versa. If the machine does not run after you screw in the thumbscrew, switch holes.

SEWING AROUND A CURVE

You can use an adjustable cloth guide when sewing around a curve. Adjust the guide to match the outline of your curve and, as you sew, the fabric will touch the tip of the bottom guide.

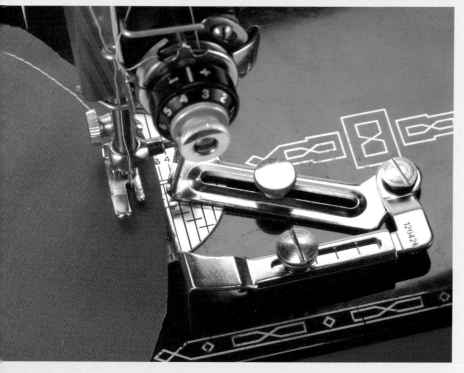

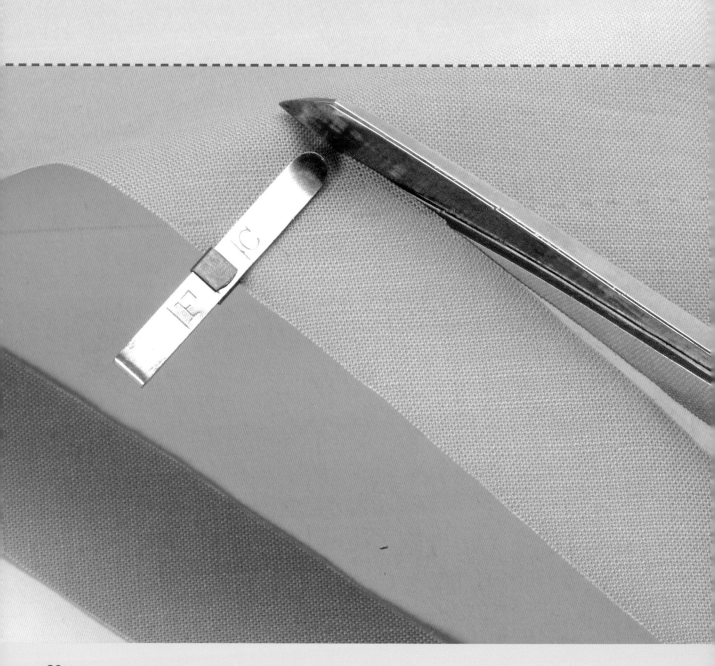

Although today you do have an abundance of commercial binding, cording and facings to choose from, when you use this handy sewing tool you can make your own binding to match your project perfectly and inexpensively. Binding can be used to trim such items as collars, baby bibs and apron pockets, working very nicely to keep edges from fraying and being decorative at the same time.

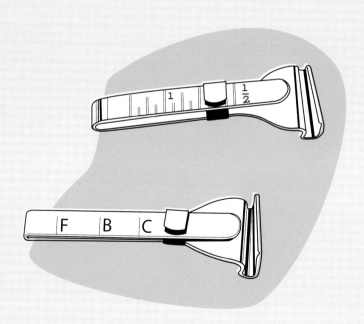

By using the bias cutting gauge, you will be able to cut even-width bias strips without any further measuring or marking. It was designed to work with your binder, letting you cut your fabric to the proper size to fit within the binder's scrolls. You can cut bias bands from about $7/16$" to $1\frac{3}{8}$" (11mm to 35mm) wide, which corresponds to the sizes necessary to work with your binder. Your cutting gauge might indicate letters that represent facings (F), binding (B) and cording (C), or it might provide measurements in inches.

Using the Bias Cutting Gauge

LOOKING BACK

The bias cutting gauge made by the Greist Manufacturing Company was called a "scissors cutting gauge," while the Singer Sewing Machine Company's was called a "bias cutting gauge."

ADJUSTING YOUR GAUGE

Slide the gauge onto the end of your scissors, adjust the blue spring to the desired width of binding you need, and begin cutting. If you slide the blue spring all the way to the left, it will give you a cutting measurement of 1⅜" (35mm). The farther you move the spring to the right, the smaller your measurement. Practice cutting bias strips of various fabric weights to use in your binder.

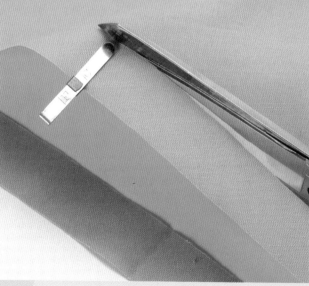

CUTTING BIAS STRIPS PROPERLY

In order to create perfect binding that lies flat when sewn and provides you with beautiful curves, your bias strips must be cut so the grain is truly diagonal, at a 45-degree angle to the selvage of your material. Determine your first bias line, press it, and begin cutting on this fold with your cutting gauge. Continue cutting bias strips until you have enough for your project.

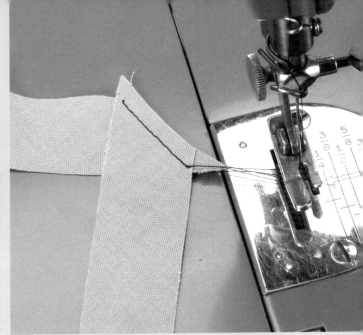

PIECING A BIAS STRIP

Always piece your bias strips so the grain in the two pieces matches. Lay them right sides together, with the ends of each piece crossing. Join the fabric on the diagonal, never straight across the binding. Sew an ⅛" (3mm) seam, and then trim the tips to create even sides. Your binding bias strip is now ready to use in your binder.

TIPS

One yard (91cm) of fabric 45" (114cm) wide will make about 30 yards (27m) of bias strips that are ⅞" (22mm) wide. For bias strips 1¼" (32mm) wide, you will get about 35 yards (32m) of bias strips.

The binder attachment has a measurement indicator engraved on the side, a visual as to the largest unfolded bias strip you can insert, which is ¹⁵/₁₆" (24mm).

If you prefer, you can create a prefolded bias strip with a bias-tape maker (see pages 45-46 for instructions). As you insert your bias strip through the maker, it will fold the strip while you press the folds. This step is certainly optional when using any binder attachment, since the binders will also accept unfolded bias strips.

The binder attachment automatically folds and places bias strips or prefolded binding over the edge of your fabric as you sew, creating a finished seam.

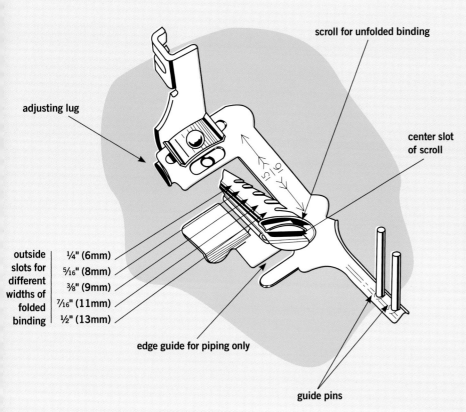

scroll for unfolded binding

adjusting lug

center slot of scroll

outside slots for different widths of folded binding

¼" (6mm)
⁵⁄₁₆" (8mm)
³⁄₈" (9mm)
⁷⁄₁₆" (11mm)
½" (13mm)

edge guide for piping only

guide pins

You may have a binder with two slots to use two different sizes of binding, or five slots allowing up to five sizes of binding. The multislotted binder will have two guide pins protruding from the end to guide the binding strip.

Binders accommodate single-fold binding and prefolded binding. Unfolded binding must measure ¹⁵⁄₁₆" (24mm) wide if it does *not* stretch, and 1" to 1¼" (25mm to 32mm) wide if it *does* stretch. This measurement is marked on the side of the binder. Folded binding is inserted into the proper side slot, while unfolded binding must be inserted into the open end of the scroll.

Using the Binder

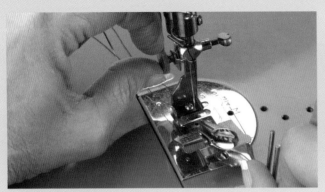

ATTACHING THE BINDER TO YOUR MACHINE
When attaching the binder to the machine in place of your regular presser foot, be sure the needle falls within the hole. Then, to adjust your binder, hold the shank of the binder by one hand, and with your other hand, move the lower part of the binder. It moves left to right to allow you to adjust where the stitching falls in relation to your material and binding. Your binder may have a small adjusting screw, which you will need to loosen before adjusting.

1

Cut a long point on the end of your bias binding strip. Begin sliding into the proper slot. Use a stiletto or small screwdriver to guide it through. Continue pushing until it comes out past your needle area. You can use tweezers to help pull it through. If you have guide pins, place the other end of your binding between the pins.

Lower the needle into the fabric to check your stitching. Move the scroll to the left or right as needed. The line of stitching will be nearer to the edge of the binding by moving the scroll to the left, and farther away by moving it to the right.

2

Place the edge of your material to be bound as far to the right as it will go between the two halves of the scroll. This is an important step to ensure your material is stitched in the center of your binding.

When sewing outside curves, guide the edge of the material toward the left, turning it while you sew. When sewing inside curves, straighten out the material edge as it enters the binder.

FRENCH FOLDS

Place your fabric and binding underneath the binder. When working from a raw edge, sew your binding to the edge first and then progress inward, adding the binding as desired.

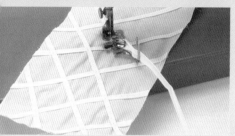

LATTICE DESIGN CREATED WITH BINDING

When using lightweight material, you may want to add a stabilizer underneath your fabric to prevent puckering.

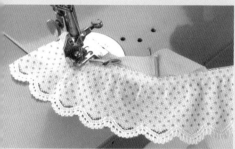

BINDING A RUFFLE EDGE

Choose a lightweight ruffle, because it inserts through the guides and under the needle more easily than a thicker, heavier ruffle.

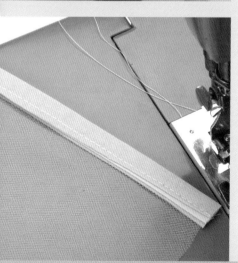

TWO-TONE BINDING

For two-tone binding, you have a variety of options for colors and sizes. Whenever combining binding sizes, always eliminate a slot between each width being used. For example, use slots for ¼" and ⅜" (6mm and 9mm), ⁵⁄₁₆" and ⁷⁄₁₆" (8mm and 11mm), or ⅜" and ½" (9mm and 13mm). For the two-tone binding, I first inserted my unfolded bias strip into the proper scroll, then both the prefolded binding and the fabric into the center scroll, with the prefolded binding folded over the raw edge.

TIPS

You can use three different bindings if you have the five-slotted binder, using slots for ¼" (6mm), ⅜" (9mm) and ½" (13mm). The last two slots give the appearance of double piping, while the ¼" (6mm) slot encloses the material and your other binding.

Sewing machine manuals might refer to the "no. 5 inch folded binding," which measures ½" (13mm) by today's standards.

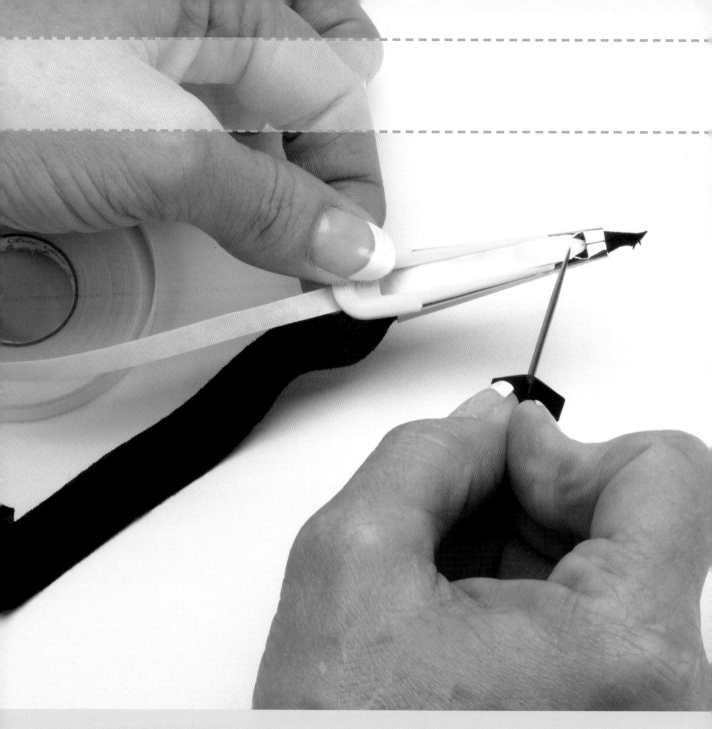

BIAS-TAPE MAKER and FUSIBLE-TAPE MAKER

A bias-tape maker is perfect for creating your own prefolded binding to match or contrast with your sewing project. You choose the fabric and the size you need. Whether adding binding to your quilt or a set of napkins, the result is truly unique. The fusible-tape maker lets you turn any fabric into heat-sensitive bias tape.

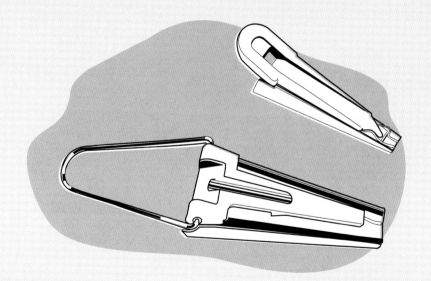

With the bias-tape maker you can make one long bias strip. Bias-tape makers come in widths of ¼" (6mm), ½" (13mm), ¾" (19mm), 1" (25mm) and 2" (51mm). Whether you have an older tape maker or a newer one, they work in similar fashion.

The fusible-tape maker has an added slot, allowing you to create fusible-bias tape at a much lower cost than commercial fusible tape. They come in widths of ¼" (6mm), ⅜" (9mm), ½" (13mm), ¾" (19mm) and 1" (25mm).

Using the Bias-Tape Maker

1

Cut your fabric into strips, remembering to cut them on a true bias. The rule is to double the width you cut in proportion to the size of the tape maker. For example, if you're using the ½" (13mm) tape maker, cut your strips into 1" (25mm) widths. You can cut the strips using a ruler and rotary cutter. If you have a bias cutting gauge, turn to pages 37–38 for instructions on how to use it.

2

After cutting the end of a strip to a nice point, insert it through the tape maker. Gently push with your stiletto.

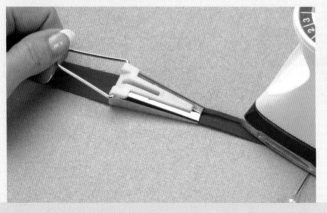

3

Pin one end of the strip onto your ironing board. Pull the tape maker while pressing the folded tape. If you are not using the bias binding right away, wind it up to maintain the fold and prevent it from stretching.

Using the Fusible-Tape Maker

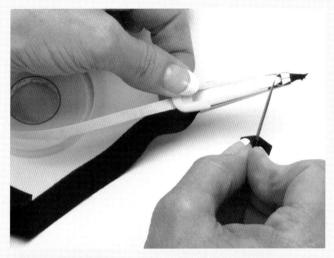

CREATING FUSIBLE BIAS BINDING

The ¼" (6mm) tape maker creates fusible binding equal to the size you might purchase. Insert your bias strip into the lower groove, as shown in step 2 on page 46, making sure to cut the tip of the fabric to a point. Cut a point on the end of your fusible web. Insert the fusible web into the upper groove with the adhesive side down. Pull the two together, using a stiletto to push through. Set your iron to medium dry heat. Pin one end of the binding to the ironing board. Pull the tape maker as you iron on the webbing. (To do this, follow step 3 on page 46.)

APPLYING THE FUSIBLE BINDING

You can create your own fusible bias binding to use when making stained glass quilts. Peel off the backing and iron the fusible binding tape to the section you wish to sew. Using the sewing machine, stitch close to both edges.

ADJUSTABLE TAPE-STITCHING PRESSER FOOT

The adjustable tape-stitching presser foot edges your fabric with varying widths of binding tape.

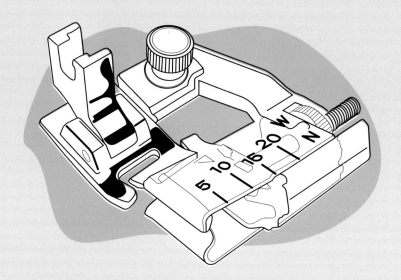

A guide adjustment screw on top of the foot works to increase or decrease the guide width, allowing you to change binding sizes without removing the foot from your sewing machine. The special guide is designed to hold your binding and fabric together securely as you stitch, ensuring your fabric is stitched properly within the folded binding.

The adjustable tape-stitching presser foot does not prepare the tape; instead it's designed to accommodate any prepared binding from ⅛" (3mm) to ¾" (19mm).

Using the Adjustable Tape-Stitching Presser Foot

ATTACHING THE ADJUSTABLE TAPE-STITCHING PRESSER FOOT TO YOUR MACHINE

Set your machine for a center, straight stitch. Replace your regular presser foot with the adjustable tape-stitching presser foot, securing it tightly. To adjust the foot for your binding size, turn the guide adjustment screw away from you to increase the width or toward you to decrease it.

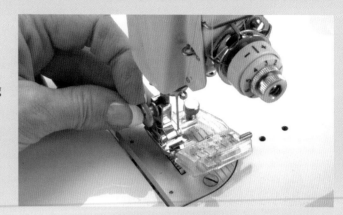

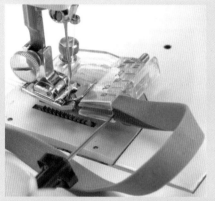

1

Cut a 45-degree angle on one end of the binding tape. Insert your tape from the corner and turn it back toward the back of the presser bar. Ensure the top fold is in the top slit and the bottom fold in the bottom slit. Adjust the guide opening with the screw until the edges of your binding tape are just touching the left side of the guide.

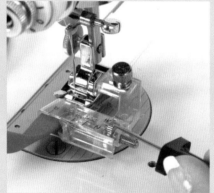

2

Adjust the position of the tape guide. Loosen the stitch position adjustment screw and adjust the position of the tape guide to place the cloth in position to be stitched.

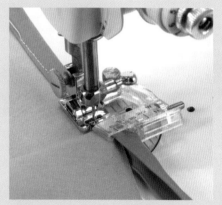

3

Lower your needle with your stitching against the edge of the bias tape. Readjust as needed. Place your material to be taped, and tighten all screws as necessary. Hold the tape and the cloth with your hands, one in front of and one behind the presser bar, and begin sewing.

SEWING BUTTON LOOPS

Making your own button loops with the adjustable tape-stitching presser foot adds a personal touch to your garment. You can easily match or contrast your loops to your fabric color. Try creating your button loops from silk.

1. Determine the binding length needed by multiplying the length of each loop by the number of loops. Insert the binding tape as previously instructed on page 50. Adjust your stitching as close to the edges as possible and begin sewing your binding into a closed fold.

2. Cut a strip of your prepared binding long enough for your button loop, plus 1" (25mm).

3. Bring the two stitched edges together and fold to a point, keeping the edges even. Tack the raw edges together. To sew onto your garment, determine the placement you want and sew the loop between the layers of your fabrics.

SEWING BINDING AND RICKRACK TO THE EDGE OF FABRIC

Using the adjustable tape-stitching presser foot, you can add both binding and rickrack to the edge of your fabric for a decorative finish on an apron or a child's dress. Prepare your adjustable tape-stitching presser foot as necessary for your binding size. Insert the fabric to be edged and insert the rickrack on top of this material. The foot will hold your binding securely, while you ensure that the fabric and rickrack are seated firmly against the guide. Lace will also work nicely.

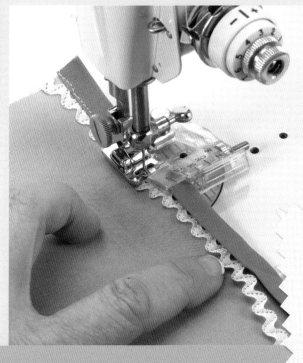

TIP

After adding a new attachment, always test your stitches. This not only allows you to check your tension, but it brings the top thread back underneath your attachment, eliminating snarled thread at the beginning of your seam.

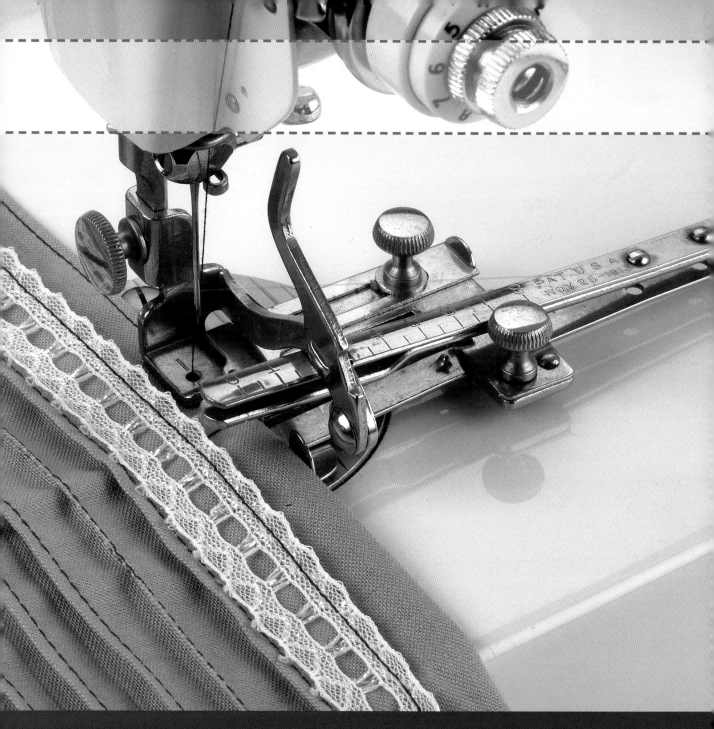

Tucks are folds used to hold fullness in place. They can be decorative as well as functional.

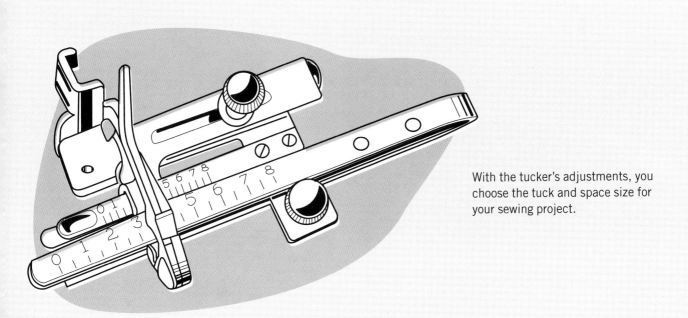

With the tucker's adjustments, you choose the tuck and space size for your sewing project.

Using the Tucker

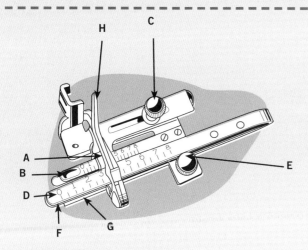

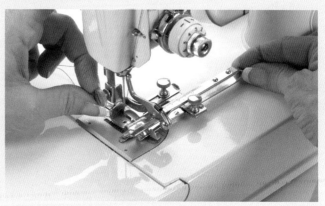

PARTS OF THE TUCKER

A Tuck Guide: adjustable for any desired width of tuck

B Tuck Scale: numbers indicate the width of the tucks. The tuck scale also acts as a smoother blade, keeping tucks a uniform width

C Tuck Guide Adjusting Screw: sets the tuck guide

D Space Scale: numbers on the upper blade indicate the width of the space between tucks. The grooved blade has a groove where the fabric is pressed by the spur blade, marking the fabric for the folding of your next tuck

E Space Scale Adjusting Screw: sets the space scale

F Grooved Blade: has a groove which the spur blade fits into

G Spur Blade: comes exactly into the center of the grooved blade to mark the next tuck

H Marking Lever: presses on the grooved blade, marking the material as it passes between the grooved and spur blades

ATTACHING THE TUCKER TO YOUR MACHINE

Check that the needle enters the center of the hole. Ensure that the marking lever is in the down position and moves up and down, marking the fabric for the next tuck.

Insert your fabric between these two blades.

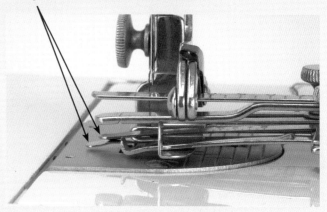

WHERE TO PLACE YOUR FABRIC

Place your fabric between the grooved blade and the spur blade. Keep the fabric against the guide bar. If your tucker is not leaving marks, gently bend the spur blade. The heavier the fabric, the fainter the mark will be.

SEWING PIN TUCKS
To create pin tucks, set the tuck guide at 1 and set the space scale at 1½.

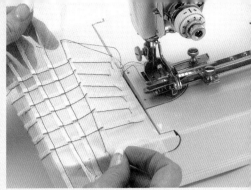

CROSS TUCKS
Create your tucks lengthwise. Carefully iron the tucks in one direction. Then create crosswise tucks at a 90-degree angle to the initial tucks.

ADJUSTING TUCKS

The numbers on the tuck scale indicate the tuck width in eighths of an inch; the marks between the figures are sixteenths. The marks on the space scale are double the width of those on the tuck scale. When both scales are set at the same figure, blind tucks without spaces are made.

To make the space between the tucks, set the tuck scale, and then move the space scale to the same number and as much farther to the left as you wish to have your space. For example, set tuck scale at 2, move your space scale to 2 and then farther left to the size of the space between the tucks.

To regulate the tucker, loosen the tuck guide adjusting screw and move the guide to the desired number. Tighten the screw.

To adjust for the width of space between the tucks, loosen the space scale adjusting screw and move the space scale until the number is directly in a line with the center of the needle hole. There is a line on the tucker in front and back of the needle hole to indicate the center. Tighten the screw.

	TUCK GUIDE	SPACE SCALE
⅛" (3mm) tucks with no space	1	1
⅛" (3mm) tucks with ⅛" space	1	1½
¼" (6mm) tucks with no space	2	2
¼" (6mm) tucks with ¼" space	2	3
½" (13mm) tucks with no space	4	4
½" (13mm) tucks with ½" space	4	6
1" (25mm) tucks with no space	8	8

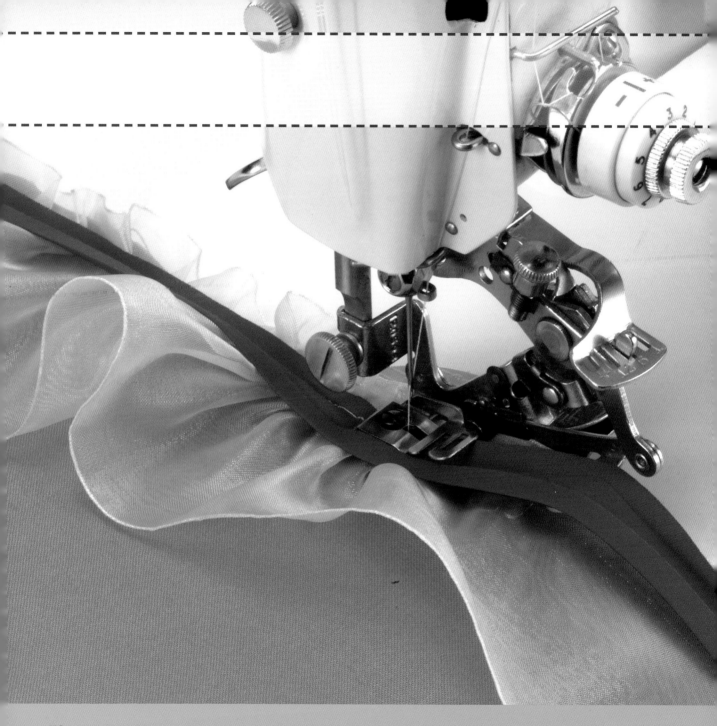

Your ruffler creates ruffling and pleating in uniform fullness or, with simple adjustments, groupings of gathers or pleats. Adjustments are made without removing the ruffler from the machine.

There are several types of rufflers. Some are controlled by a thumbscrew located on the top, and others are controlled by moving a lever into a number slot. You may have either a dial or a thumbscrew on the side of your ruffler. Regardless of the type you have, there are two controlling areas: the top and the side. The fullness of the gathers or width of the pleats will also be controlled by your stitch length.

Over the years there have been many variations of rufflers (see illustration). The number of stitches refers to the pleat spacing, which determines the depth of your ruffles. The ruffler with 1 stitch doesn't have a projection lever to adjust pleating spaces; instead it's controlled by a screw on the top of the machine. The farther you turn the screw to the right while facing the machine, the fuller the gathers and the narrower the spacing of pleats.

1, 6, 12 stitches (with screw on top)

1, 6, 12 stitches (without screw on top)

1, 5 stitches

1 stitch (controlled by lever at side)

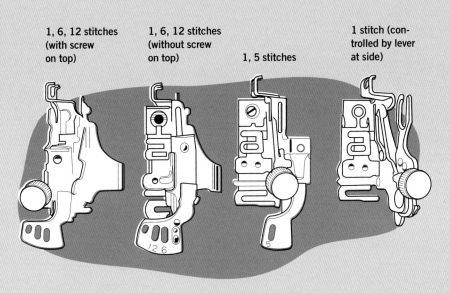

Using the Ruffler

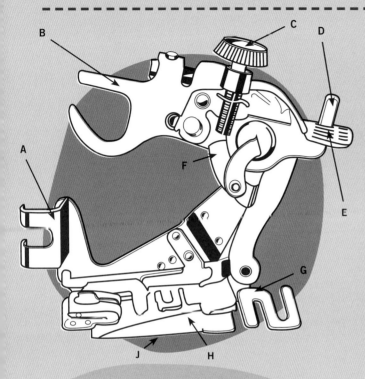

PARTS OF THE RUFFLER

A Foot: attaches to the presser bar in place of the normal presser foot

B Fork Arm: straddles the needle clamp (this requires a little maneuvering)

C Adjusting Screw: regulates the fullness of the gathers

D Projection Lever: projects through the slots in the adjusting lever (lift and move)

E Adjusting Lever: sets the ruffler for gathering or making a pleat every 6 inches (15cm) or every 12 inches (30cm), as you wish. This also can disengage the ruffler when gathering or pleating is not wanted

F Adjusting Finger: regulates the width or the size of your pleats

G Separator Guide: (on the bottom of the ruffler) contains slots into which the edge of the fabric is placed to keep the heading of the ruffle even. It also keeps the fabric to be ruffled separate from the fabric on which you are placing the ruffle

H Ruffling Blade: (upper blue blade, with teeth at the end) pushes the fabric in pleats up to the needle

J Separator Blade: (lower blue blade) prevents the teeth of the ruffling blade from coming into contact with the feed of your machine or your fabric

LOOKING BACK

In 1874, John M. Griest applied for and received a patent for a "ruffling and gathering" attachment. In 1884, Mr. Griest improved on this invention and assigned the patent to the Singer Manufacturing Company. In 1892, John M. Greist (with a new spelling for his name) improved the ruffler again, but this time the patent was assigned to the Greist Manufacturing Company.

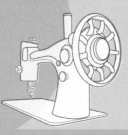

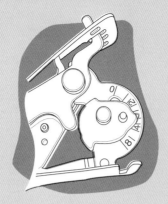

ATTACHING THE RUFFLER TO YOUR MACHINE

Raise the needle bar to its highest point and remove the presser foot. Attach the ruffler foot to the bar while placing the fork arm astride the needle clamp. Ensure the needle enters the center of the hole.

ADJUSTING THE DIAL GAUGE

Some rufflers have a dial gauge below the projection lever. When the pointer is all the way up, it doesn't create any gathers. Move the pointer downward and your gathering begins. Higher numbers produce more fullness; lower numbers produce less. A very deep pleat can be obtained with a setting of 8.

TIP

To make fine gathering, shorten the stroke of the ruffling blade by turning the adjusting screw (C) upward and shortening your stitch length. To make fuller gathering, lengthen the stroke of the ruffling blade by turning the adjusting screw downward and increasing your stitch length.

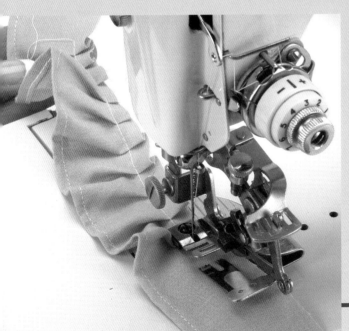

MAKING A PLAIN GATHER

Place the projection lever in slot number 1. If you wish to create pleating, place the lever in either slot 12 or 5, depending on the number of stitches of your ruffler. Place your ruffling material as shown.

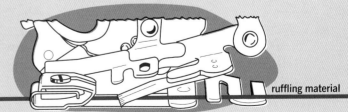

ruffling material

MAKING A RUFFLE AND SEWING IT
TO THE BASE FABRIC IN ONE STEP

Place the fabric for the ruffle between the two blue blades and insert the fabric it will be attached to under the separator blade.

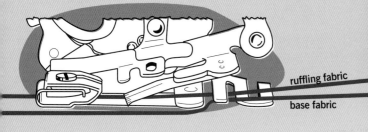

ruffling fabric

base fabric

MAKING A RUFFLE AND ATTACHING
IT WITH FACING IN ONE STEP

Insert the fabric to be ruffled between the two blue blades. Place the fabric the ruffle will be sewn to under the separator blade. Place the facing material over the upper blue blade.

If your facing is to be on the right side of garment, place the wrong sides of the garment and ruffle together.

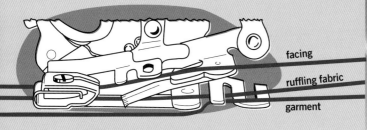

facing

ruffling fabric

garment

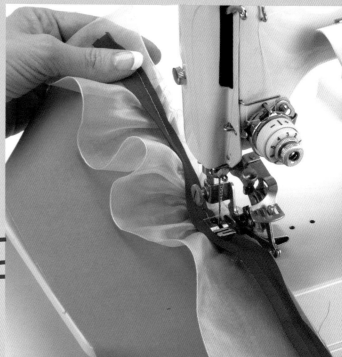

APPLYING ROWS OF RUFFLES

With your ruffler, you can apply rows of gathers directly to your fabric, wherever you want. Rows of ruffles can be sewn onto your fabric at the same time the material is ruffled. Place your base fabric under the ruffler and the fabric to be ruffled between the blades.

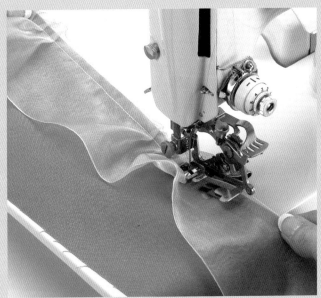

PLEATING

Place the projection lever in slot 12 or 5, depending on the ruffler. Turn the adjusting screw down as far as it will go. To control the distance between your pleats, either lengthen or shorten your machine's stitch length. Just as with ruffles, pleats can be made and sewn to your fabric in one step. Place your base fabric under the blades and the fabric to be pleated between the two blue blades.

GROUP PLEATING OR GROUP RUFFLING

Lift the projection lever and place it in the slot indicated by the star (see photo at left). Do this whenever you want to sew straight stitching between the pleats; your ruffler will stop pleating and sew a straight stitch. When you wish to continue your pleats, stop sewing and return the projection lever into the slot number you were using previously.

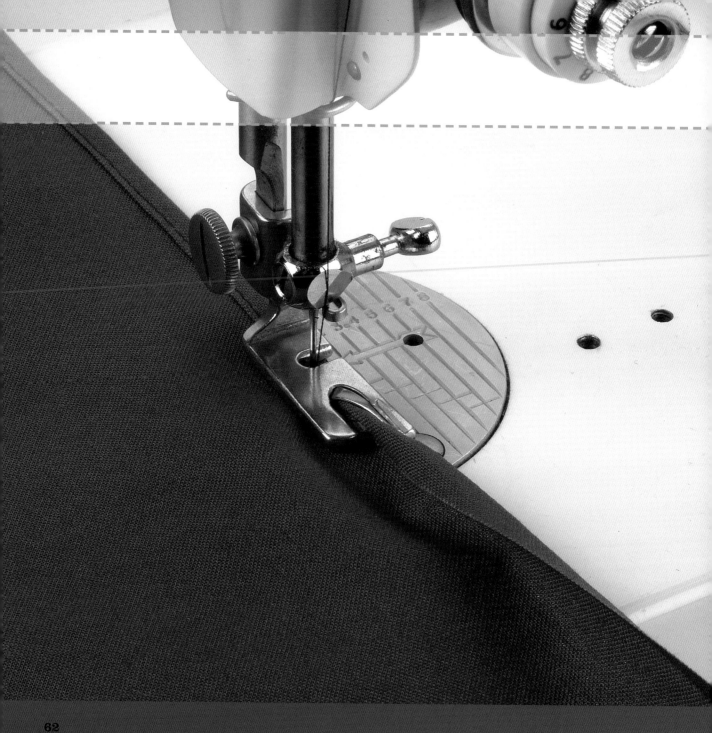

The foot hemmer is used for hemming the edge of the fabric, as well as for making hemmed and felled seams. You can also use your foot hemmer to hem and sew on lace in just one operation.

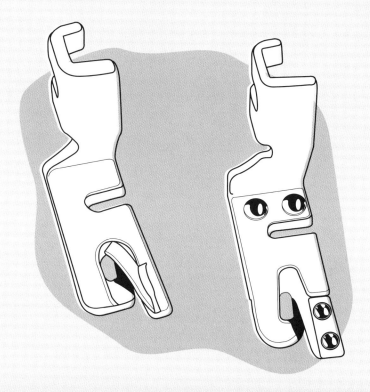

The foot hemmer has a spiral tongue (scroll) that turns in the edge of the fabric and forms the hem. It is attached to your machine in place of the regular presser foot. Foot hemmers come in varying sizes, such as ⅛" (3mm), ¼" (6mm) and ⁵⁄₆₄" (2mm).

Using the Foot Hemmer

ATTACHING THE FOOT HEMMER TO YOUR MACHINE

Raise your needle to the highest position, remove your regular presser foot and attach the foot hemmer. Always be sure to tighten the thumbscrew all the way.

Closeup of the hemmer's scroll

1

To prepare to hem, first fold the edge of your fabric twice, about ⅛" (3mm) each time. Do this for a distance of about 2" (51mm) and finger-crease the fold.

Place the creased edge of your fabric under the hemmer, having the hem edge directly under the needle. The bottom of your hem will be even with the right edge of the hemmer. Lower the hemmer foot and take about two or three stitches.

2

Raise the hemmer. Pull the threads and the hem slightly away from you with your left hand (while holding the threads), and pull the fabric in front of the hemmer toward you with your right hand; fitting it into the scroll of the hemmer until the tacked end is nestled within the hemmer. Move it back and forth gently until the fabric is within the scroll of the hemmer foot.

3

Lower the hemmer and begin sewing, continuing to hold the threads behind the needle. Keep the mouth of the hemmer full of fabric so you will have an even hem.

SEWING A FELLED SEAM

Place the right sides of the fabric together. Do not match them at the edge; you want the upper piece of fabric about ⅛" (3mm) to the left of the fabric on the bottom. Stitch the two pieces together using the hemmer-foot toe as your sewing guide. Open the seam wrong side up, flatten it and begin hemming, stitching it flat. Use the toe as your sewing guide.

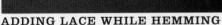

ADDING LACE WHILE HEMMING

To hem and sew on lace in one step, begin as for hemming. Raise the presser foot and insert the edge of your lace into the slot of the hemmer, pulling it back under the hemmer.

    The needle will catch the lace on the edge of your hem. Guide the fabric being hemmed with your left hand while guiding the lace with your right. This keeps it within the slot and directly above the hem. Ensure your needle stitches through both the lace and the hem.

LOOKING BACK

In 1861, a patent was applied for and assigned to the Wheeler & Wilson Manufacturing Company for an "improvement in hemming guide." In 1892, Russell S. Barnum of Illinois applied for a patent for a hemmer that attached to the bed plate instead of the presser foot. The received patent was assigned to Frank L. Goodrich.

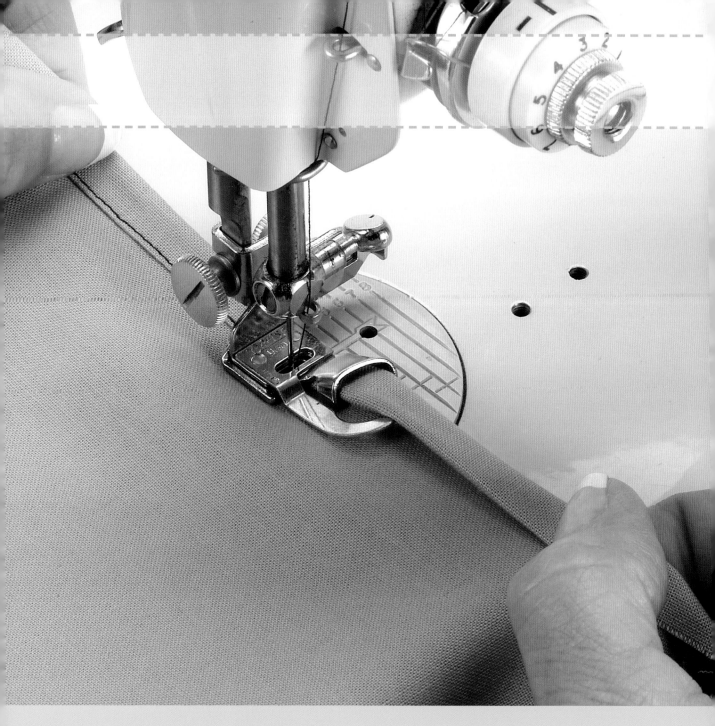

HEMMER SET

The hemmer set takes the place of measuring, creasing, pinning and basting a hem, while producing straight, even stitches.

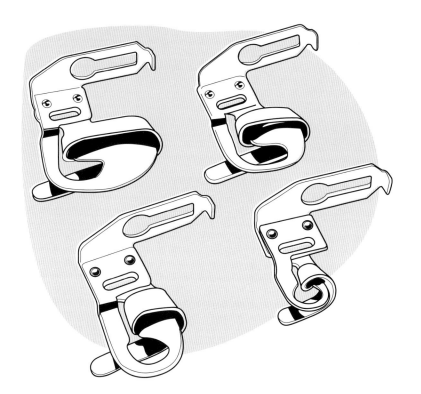

Sew your hem with matching thread or, for a more decorative finish, use a contrasting color. A set of four hemmers will finish hems ¼" (6mm), ⅜" (9mm), ⅝" (16mm) and ⅞" (22mm). The smallest is a linen hemmer, creating a narrow hem suitable for napkins. The largest produces a wide hem appropriate for tablecloths or draperies.

Using the Hemmers

 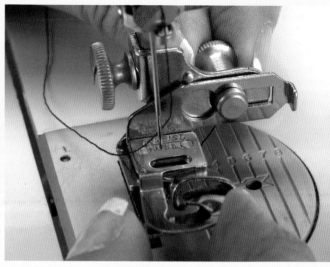

ATTACHING A HEMMER TO YOUR MACHINE

The attachment foot (page 28) must replace the regular presser foot when using a hemmer. Press the blue spring on the foot forward and slip the large hole in the hemmer over the rivet on the attachment foot. If your foot has a thumbscrew, loosen the screw and press the thumbscrew, sliding the large hole in the hemmer over the rivet. Tighten it securely.

To change the hem width, remove the hemmer from the attachment foot and replace it with a different size. You do not have to remove the attachment foot from your presser bar to change hemmers.

MAKING ADJUSTMENTS

To adjust where the stitching falls on your hem, loosen the spring (or thumbscrew) and slide the foot left or right as needed.

TIPS

To prepare your article for hemming, be sure the hem has been cut evenly all the way around. This will prevent the hem from twisting and puckering.

To prepare a hem on your table linen for hand sewing, run the cloth through the hemmer, without thread. Your hem will be turned, creased and ready to hand sew.

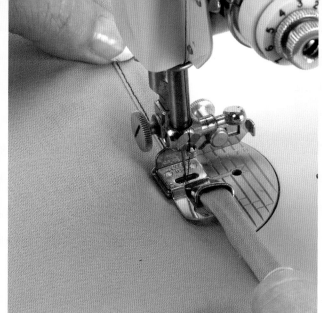

1

Insert the fabric to be hemmed between the narrow, horizontal band and the rounded scroll, pulling it up and over the rounded scroll, and letting it fold under the top scroll. When you insert your material, hold it in both hands and move it back and forth a few times. This will create an initial pressed fold and ensure the hemmer scroll is completely and properly filled.

2

When the hemmer scroll is properly filled, you will have an ⅛" (3mm) fold of the raw edge, and your hem width will be within the scroll. Lower your presser foot and begin sewing. Guide the material gently to keep the scroll filled. If too little is fed into the hemmer, the raw edges won't be turned; if too much enters the scroll, you will have an uneven hem. Just the right amount of fabric should be caught in your stitching. If necessary, stop and readjust.

LOOKING BACK

The hemmer set was originally part of an attachment set that included an attachment foot, cloth guide, adjustable zipper foot, scissors cutting gauge, gathering foot, narrow foot hemmer, edge stitcher, multiple-slotted binder and ruffler. Invented by John M. Greist, the set was sold with many machine models, including the Kenmore sewing machine sold by Sears, Roebuck and Company.

A new attachment foot is available for most sewing machines in low, high and slant shank.

ADJUSTABLE HEMMER

The adjustable hemmer allows you to sew a variety of hem widths, all using a single attachment.

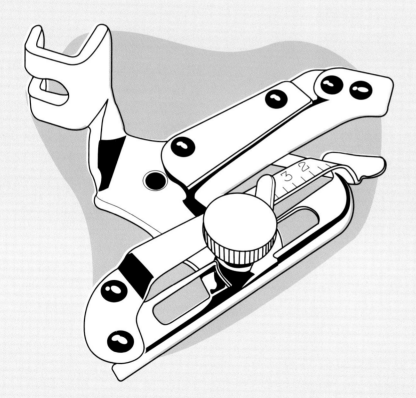

The adjustable hemmer was part of the set of attachments supplied with many sewing machines. Hemmers are invaluable, useful for kitchen or hand towels, edges of ruffles, aprons and bonnet strings, and readying your table linen for hand sewing.

With its scale closed, the attachment creates hems up to 1" (25mm) wide. For hems of a wider width, the scale may be released and "thrown out of position."

Using the Adjustable Hemmer

ATTACHING THE ADJUSTABLE HEMMER TO YOUR MACHINE

Remove your presser foot and attach the hemmer to the presser bar. Be sure the needle falls within the center of the needle hole.

ADJUSTING THE HEMMER

To adjust the hemmer, loosen the screw and move the hemmer guide to the right or to the left. Notice the pointer used with the scale number. Set the pointer for your desired hem width.

LOOKING BACK

Black hemmers were produced during the war years when materials such as chromium, nickel and aluminum were at a premium. You may have a hemmer that is part silver and part black. As new parts were made, they were dumped into bins that already contained parts made with different materials. When the assembler reached into the bin for a part, he or she simply used whichever was pulled out first.

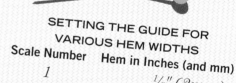

SETTING THE GUIDE FOR VARIOUS HEM WIDTHS

Scale Number	Hem in Inches (and mm)
1	⅛" (3mm)
2	¼" (6mm)
3	⅜" (9mm)
4	½" (13mm)
5	⅝" (16mm)
6	¾" (19mm)
7	⅞" (22mm)
8	1" (25mm)

SEWING A HEM

Choose your hem width by setting your pointer on the scale and tighten the screw. To prepare your fabric for hemming, insert it and fold over the edge to be hemmed about ⅛" (3mm), and then finger press. Place the fabric under the scale and draw it back and forth until a hem is formed. You can now determine the width and fold the hem over for the second turning.

Draw the cloth back until the end comes directly under the needle. Lower the presser bar and begin sewing, continuously guiding enough material into the hemmer to produce an even hem. If the hem is not started correctly, it will twist and become uneven at the end.

FOR A WIDER HEM

To make a hem more than 1" (25mm) wide, loosen the adjusting screw, draw the slide to the right as far as it will go and turn it toward you, throwing the scale guide out of position. Attach it to your presser bar in the normal way. Fold and crease down a hem of the desired width, pass the fold under the extension at the right of the hemmer, insert the edge of the fabric into the folder and begin sewing. The hemmer will turn the edge and stitch it flat; however, for larger hems you must continue to fold and keep the hem creased as you sew.

TIP

When hemming soft fabrics that may stretch, you can slip a piece of paper or interfacing under the hemmer next to the feed dogs. This will prevent the material from stretching and assist in turning your hem.

The edge stitcher keeps seams straight when you're sewing laces, inserting embroidery or creating piped edges.

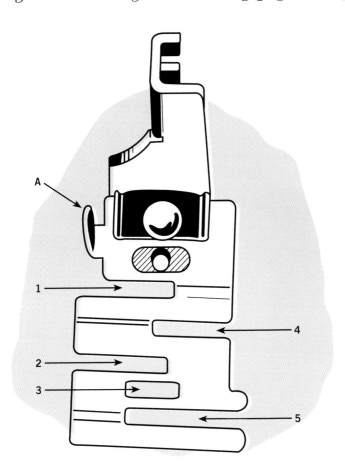

The advantage of using the edge stitcher is the versatility of the slots on each side. You can determine which slots you wish to use, depending upon the weight of your materials and how close you wish the stitching line to be on each edge. The slots on the edge stitcher are numbered from 1 to 5 and are used as your guides. Regardless of the slots used in the photos on the following pages, you can easily choose different slots to serve your purpose.

To adjust your stitching line, the edge stitcher has a lug (A). Loosen this lug and move the attachment left or right as necessary.

Using the Edge Stitcher

ATTACHING THE EDGE STITCHER TO YOUR MACHINE

Raise the presser bar to the highest point, remove your presser foot and attach the edge stitcher. Be sure your needle goes through the hole and does not hit the plate.

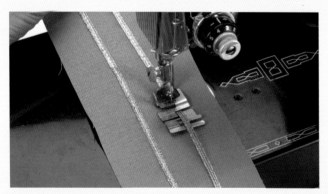

SEWING ON BRAIDS

For a tailored trim, use the edge stitcher to sew on braids. Mark a guideline for the trimming using a marking pencil. Insert the braid in slot 4 and adjust to sew close to the edge of the braid. Place the fabric to be trimmed under the edge stitcher. Add as many rows of braids as you want, depending on the look you desire.

SEWING TWO PIECES OF LACE TOGETHER

Place one edge in slot 1. Adjust the lug so the stitch will be close to the edge. Place your second piece of lace in slot 4. Keep the pieces slightly overlapped as you sew. Gently hold the fabric both behind and in front of the edge stitcher. If the lace begins to pucker, check the tension on your sewing machine. You can continue to add rows of lace, or possibly an embroidered insert, creating an heirloom garment.

TIP

If you find it hard to adjust the edge stitcher, place a drop of oil on the blue spring. You may have to push fairly hard several times until it loosens.

SEWING ON A RUFFLE WHILE HEMMING

To add a ruffle while hemming a garment with the edge stitcher, turn your hem over about ¼" (6mm) and place the folded hem in slot 1 and the ruffle in slot 4. Begin sewing.

The same method can be used to insert lace between two pieces of fabric or for finishing the edge of the garment without making a hem. Try adding some vintage cream lace to your dresses for a feminine 1940s look. Inserting lace between two edges provides an immediate finish without fussy hemming.

TIPS

Your edge stitcher will also create beautiful French seams. Use your regular presser foot to make the first line of stitching. Place the fabric edges together, sewing the first line of stitching on the right side of the material. Remove the presser foot and attach the edge stitcher. Place the folded edge in slot 2 and adjust the lug for the width of seam you desire.

For a wide hem, measure and turn the edge, slightly pressing it. Insert the edge of the hem into slot 5. Adjust the edge stitcher to bring the stitching line close to the edge of the hem.

SEWING ON PIPING

Piping provides a finished look that's especially pretty when using piping of contrasting color or print. To pipe, place the piping in slot 3, with the finished edge of the piping to the left and the edge to be piped in slot 4.

A gathering foot automatically gathers with each stitch the machine takes. Unlike the ruffler, the gathering foot produces only a slight fullness.

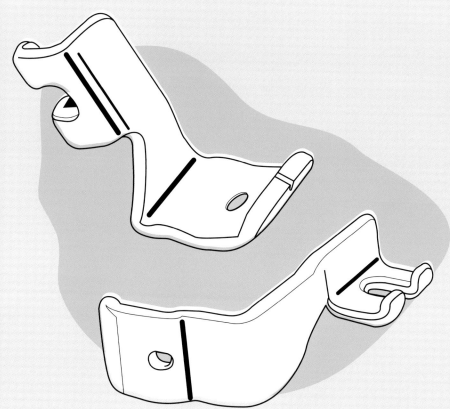

The stitch length controls the fullness of gathers. The longer the stitch, the fuller the gather, while a shorter stitch length will decrease the size of the gathers. Fine materials such as silks, net and batiste will produce fuller gathers, while heavier fabrics create only slight gathers.

The bottom of the gathering foot is specifically made to gently pull the fabric forward with each stitch. Whether you have an original attachment for your machine or a newer reproduction, each will work the same way.

Using the Gathering Foot

ATTACHING THE GATHERING FOOT TO YOUR MACHINE

Replace the presser foot with the gathering foot. Place the fabric under the gathering foot and stitch in the usual manner. Experiment with various types of material, adjusting your stitch length and tension as needed.

USING A QUILTING GUIDE

To keep your rows straight and evenly spaced when using the gathering foot, you might find it beneficial to attach a quilting guide. Attach the guide to the machine in back of the gathering foot. Loosen the thumbscrew and slip it between the foot and the screw. Tighten it securely. You can now set the quilting guide so it follows the previous row of stitching.

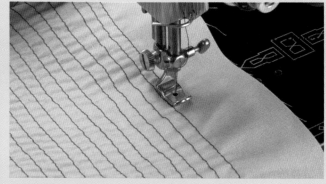

MAKING SHIRRED FABRIC

Shirring is attractive around the waist or at the top of a sleeve. Mark your shirring rows with a washable marking pen to ensure they are straight and evenly spaced. You may find it easier to begin at the left edge of your fabric and continue moving it to the outside with each new row. As you stitch the rows, you may notice the gathers from the previous row forming tiny folds in the fabric. Gently ease these folds out as you sew. Once you've created your shirred material, pin your pattern piece to it and cut accordingly.

TIP

The gathering foot is perfect for adding a little decorative touch to a garment, such as gathering the bodice of a dress. Lightly gather your fabric and then pin to your bodice pattern. To achieve a perfect fit, you have the option of pulling the machine threads at the end of your gathered material, drawing the gathers together for more fullness.

PUFFING

Puffing is a traditional, heirloom sewing technique achieved through shirred inserts.

SMOCKING

Dainty and decorative smocking can be achieved using the gathering foot. Insert several strands of embroidery floss through the needle hole of the gathering foot and stitch to the material while gathering. Gently move the embroidery floss left to right as you sew. This allows your straight-stitch sewing machine to securely catch the embroidery floss with each stitch. Another decorative effect can be achieved by using embroidery silk or heavy-duty thread in a contrasting color as the bobbin thread.

ELASTIC SHIRRING

Some patterns may require elastic shirring. Elastic thread is hand wound onto the bobbin without stretching. Hold the thread loosely in your hand while winding to prevent stretching. Do not use your machine's bobbin winder. Before sewing, set your stitch regulator to a longer stitch length, and loosen the tension just a bit.

DOUBLE SHIRRING FOOT

The difference between the gathering foot and the double shirring foot is the side slit in the latter, which allows you to easily gather or shirr your fabric while simultaneously attaching the gather to your garment.

In contrast to gathering, where fullness is controlled within a seam, the fullness of shirring is controlled over a wide span of fabric. Shirring is formed with multiple rows of gathering and is generally done with the grain of the fabric.

Many decorative effects can be accomplished with your double shirring foot, such as an insert or a section of your yoke. Allover shirring on the front of a blouse can be achieved by using soft fabrics, such as batiste or silk. Want to add just a small amount of shirring to your garment? Add a shirred pocket or a touch of shirring at the neckline.

Using the Double Shirring Foot

 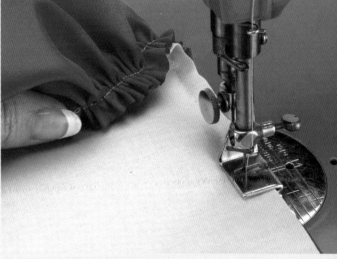

ATTACHING THE DOUBLE SHIRRING FOOT TO YOUR MACHINE
Raise the presser bar to the highest point. Replace the presser foot with the double shirring foot.

GATHERING AND SEWING THE GATHER ONTO FABRIC SIMULTANEOUSLY
To simply gather your fabric, place it directly under the shirring foot. To gather one piece of fabric and sew the gather onto your garment at the same time, place your second fabric into the slot on the side of the foot.

TIP

To space your shirring evenly, you can either use your quilting guide or pull threads from your material on the crosswise grain at 1" (25mm) intervals, or whatever spacing you desire. Shirr the fabric on each of the lines where the thread was drawn. If you lay your shirred material on a damp sheet and pin at the intervals, the fabric will be "blocked" once it dries, and will be ready for cutting according to your favorite pattern.

WAFFLE SHIRRING

Waffle shirring gives smooth fabrics, such as cotton, rayon and silk, a textured look that provides an interesting contrast to the rest of your garment or household item. To achieve the waffle effect, gather first on the crosswise and then on the lengthwise grain of your material.

TIP

Very lightweight fabrics allow fuller gathers; heavier cottons produce slighter gathers. To test your fabric for potential gathers before shirring, use a straight pin. Poke the pin in and out several times lengthwise along the edge of your fabric. If gathers fall smoothly, you can achieve fuller shirring. If the fabric stands stiffly, your shirring will be less noticeable.

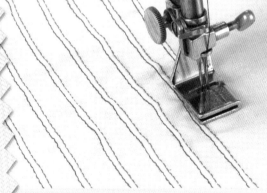

SEWING TWO ROWS OF GATHERED STITCHES AT ONE TIME

If your sewing machine has the ability to sew with double (twin) needles, you can use the double shirring foot to make two rows of gathered stitches at one time. You might also stitch along one edge of lace or other trim. Try sewing in the middle of gathered lace for an entirely different effect.

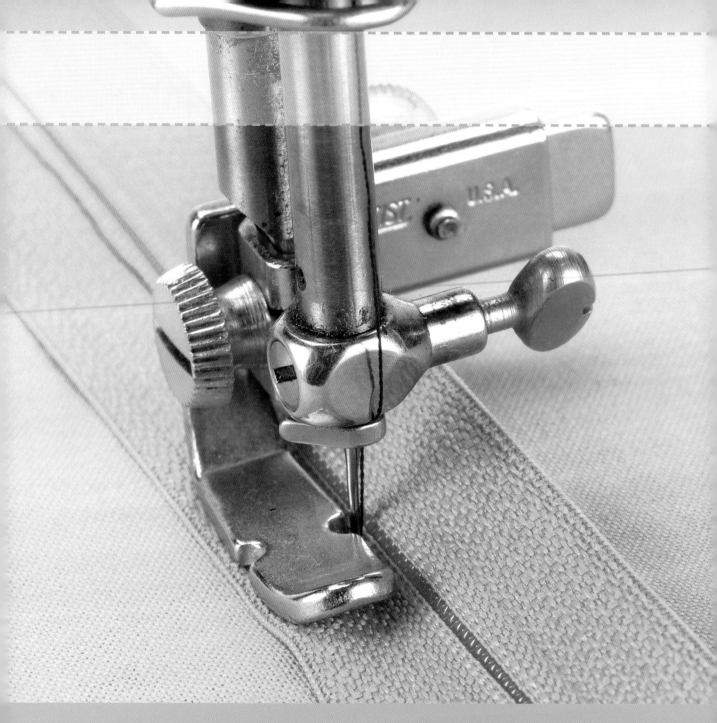

ADJUSTABLE ZIPPER/ CORDING FOOT

The adjustable zipper/cording foot allows you to insert a zipper or cover cotton filler cord with the stitching to the right or the left of the needle.

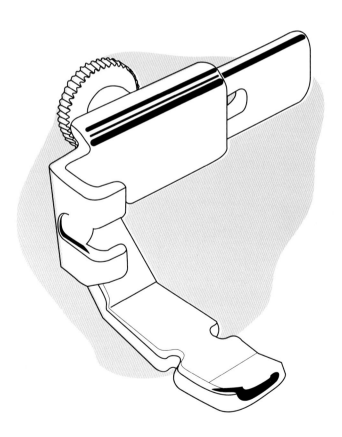

This foot is designed to ride close to the bulk without the risk of piercing the cord or zipper with the needle. Its adjustable design allows you to cover cotton filler cord of any size. Because it allows you to sew on either the left or the right, the adjustable zipper/cording foot can help you insert a zipper without turning the fabric.

Using the Adjustable Zipper/Cording Foot

ATTACHING THE ADJUSTABLE ZIPPER/ CORDING FOOT TO YOUR MACHINE

Remove your regular presser foot and attach the zipper/ cording foot. To adjust for left or right sewing, turn the thumbscrew located at the rear of the foot, moving the foot so the needle enters through the correct slot.

COVERING CORDING

Place the foot against the cording, but not so close that you might sew through it. Usually your stitching line will fall a little away from the cord when you are covering cording that will be applied to another piece of fabric (welting). This keeps the first line of stitching covered when you enclose the cording between two fabrics.

FOR A DECORATIVE FINISH ON NECKLINES

Place the cord in the center of the bias strip and fold the strip around the cord. Place the fabric, wrong side up, over the covered cord with all raw edges together. Stitch close to the cord.

TERMS TO KNOW

Cording *means to furnish, bind or connect with a cord. It is uncovered, like a fine-gauge rope.* Welting *is covered cording, usually fairly heavy, used for bulky applications.* Piping *is a trimming stitched in seams or along edges. Piping may be a fine-gauge covered cord, or it may be a rounded bias trim with no inner cord at all when used on finer applications such as around a blouse collar.*

To make simple welting, cover your cord with a strip of fabric. This strip must be cut on the true bias in order for the welting to lie flat when going around a curve. Cut a strip about 1¼" (31mm) plus three times the width of the cord, using either matching or contrasting fabric.

To enclose the cording, adjust your zipper/cording foot so you can stitch from the right side of the cord and close to the outside edge. It is best to have one continuous piece of welting ready before you begin to sew it onto your item.

For corded seams, fold a bias strip around the cord and insert the cord between your two pieces of fabric. Place all raw edges together and the right sides of the fabric together. Stitch close to the cord.

When sewing with cording, place a small piece of tape on the ends to prevent fraying. This can also be done before cutting your cord. Place a piece of tape around the cord where you plan to cut. Cut in the middle of the tape. Each end of the cord will then be protected from fraying.

1

When sewing in a skirt zipper, attach the zipper/cording foot to the presser bar. Open the zipper. Place it face down on the seam allowance with the edge of the teeth at the seam line. Stitch to the seam allowance alongside the zipper.

2

When you come to the bottom of the zipper, make several horizontal stitch lines across the tabs. Raise the zipper foot and adjust it to sew on the other side. Lower the foot and begin sewing the other side of the zipper.

Open the zipper as you sew. When you near the bottom, keep your needle in the fabric and raise the presser foot. You can now close the zipper partway, keeping the pull tab out of the way of your stitching. Repeat for the other side.

The difference between the welting foot and the adjustable zipper/ cording foot is the groove underneath the foot, which directs the cording and keeps it securely in place.

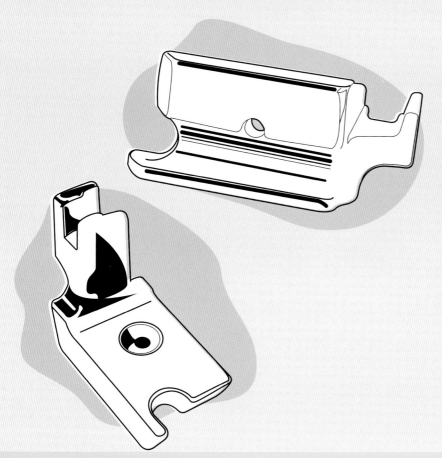

The welting foot covers cording of varying sizes. The foot comes in ⅛" (3mm), ¼" (6mm), ⅜" (9mm) and ½" (13mm) sizes. You will need to purchase the correct size foot to match your cording size. The ½" (13mm) welting foot is appropriate when sewing large, decorative welting on curtains, pillows or bedcovers. Try the dainty ¼" (6mm) size around collars, children's clothes or handbags.

Using the Welting Foot

ATTACHING THE WELTING FOOT TO YOUR MACHINE

Raise your presser bar to the highest point. Remove your regular presser foot and attach the welting foot. Be sure to tighten the thumbscrew securely. Check to ensure your needle falls within the hole in the foot.

Making Tubular Cording

1

Creating tubular cording to be used as trimming or as button loops can be done with any of the cording/welting attachments. Trim the end of the fabric strip into a point. Find the halfway point of the cording and sew the cording to the tip of the fabric lengthwise, about ½" (13mm). Sew to the wrong side of the bias strip.

2

Turn the pointed end and the continuous piece of cord to the right side of the bias strip.

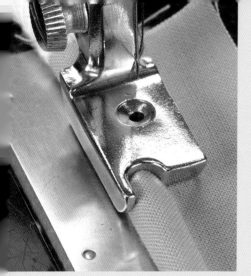

WELTING FOR A PILLOW SEAM

To create welting for a pillow seam, you can use $^6/_{32}$" (5mm) cotton filler cord and the ½" (13mm) welting foot. Cut your fabric about 4½" (11cm) in width and fold it around the cord. Place it under your welting foot, ensuring that the covered cording fits nicely within the groove, and then begin sewing.

TIP

When sewing curved seams, the length of the stitch used for enclosing your welting should be a little shorter than you would use for a straight seam to accommodate the curve. On inside curves, the seam allowance will be full, and you'll need to ease the fabric into your stitches. An outside curve requires you to stretch the seam allowance. Before turning your piece to the right side, slash the curved seams to prevent puckering.

3

Bring the fabric sides together, enclosing the cord. You now have the cord and turned point falling on the outside of the folded strip, with the remaining half of the cord extending beyond the point. Place the cording and fabric into the groove of the welting foot and begin to sew. Pull the fabric taut as you sew. Use a short stitch, forming a funnel shape at the turned point and catching only the two seam edges of the bias strip.

4

One half of the cord should now be inside the bias covering, with the other half extending from the funneled end. Trim seam allowances to ⅛" (3mm). Begin working the bias strip over the extended cord while pulling the end of the enclosed cord, eventually working the fabric over to the other side of the cord.

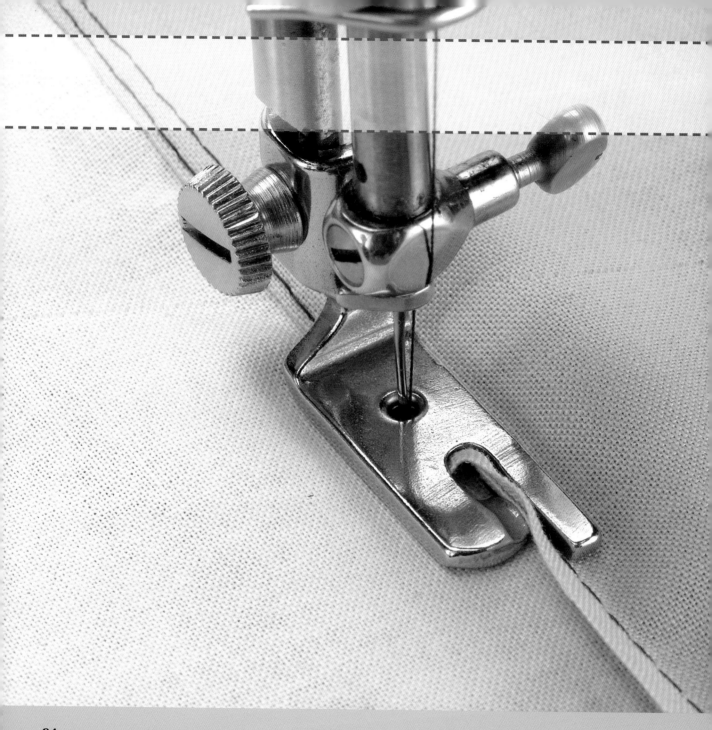

A felled seam is one wide seam allowance that is wrapped over a smaller seam allowance and then enclosed through stitching. There is a slight groove underneath the felling foot specifically designed to handle the bulk of the thicker seam and layers of fabric.

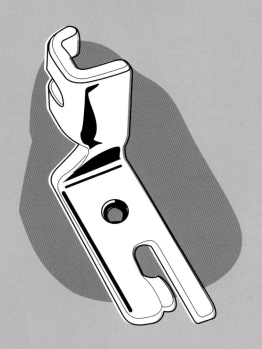

You create a felled seam by folding one raw edge under the other, and then sewing flat on the wrong side of the fabric. Felled seams are tough and durable, due to multiple lines of stitching. They are perfect for concealing raw edges or reducing the probability of fraying, for or when you need a finished narrow seam. They lend a professional finish to necklines, underarm seams or slacks. Felled seams can give skirts and blouses a sporty look, and they're perfect when making totes and travel bags.

Using the Felling Foot

ATTACHING THE FELLING FOOT TO YOUR MACHINE
Attach the felling foot to your sewing machine in place of your regular presser foot.

TIP

There are several sizes of felling feet; in general, the width between the toes of the foot is the size your finished seam will be. This measurement also acts as a guide when determining your first seam allowance. The top seam allowance will be the size of the felling foot (width between the toes), and the bottom will be twice that size. When using an ⅛" (3mm) felling foot, the top seam allowance will be ⅛" (3mm) and the bottom seam allowance will be ¼" (6mm).

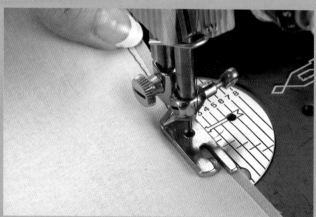

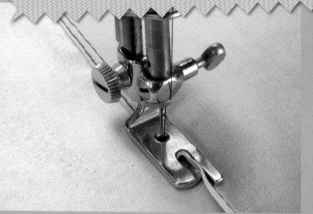

1

To make your first seam, place the pieces to be joined wrong sides together, with the bottom piece protruding about ¼" (6mm) to the right of the top seam allowance. You are matching your future stitching lines, not the raw edges. You can align the outermost edge of the bottom piece with the outermost edge of the felling foot. Sew your first stitching line.

2

With the narrower seam allowance facing you, fold the wider one over the narrower. Finger press the seam. Place the seam under the felling foot, lift the wider edge over the inside of the felling foot and sew. Your seam will be to the right of the needle. As you sew, the fabric's raw edge is folded and turned under by the foot. Guide the fabric, keeping it folded over before it gets to the toe of the felling foot.

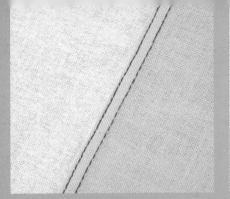

VISIBLE SEAM LINES
A felled seam has two seam lines visible on one side and one seam line visible on the other. When you place your fabric wrong sides together for your first stitching line, you will have two visible lines on the right side of your garment. If you wish to see only one seam line, place right sides together.

Alternative Method for Making a Felled Seam

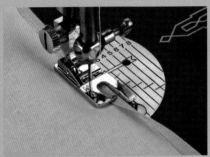
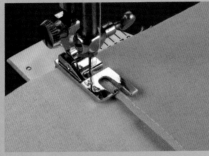

1
Pin your two pieces of fabric together, one on top of the other, so the lower piece extends about ¼" (6mm) beyond the top piece. Fold this edge over the upper piece, slide it under the felling foot and sew a couple of stitches. Leaving the needle in the work, raise the foot, guide the fabric into the toes of the foot and continue sewing. Guide your fabric as it enters the felling foot. You will then have a single fold, encasing the shorter fabric. Your stitching will have sewn onto a *raw* edge.

2
Finger press the seam open. With your fabric facing you, fold the seam over to the left. Lower the felling foot and take a couple of stitches.

3
Raise the foot and guide your fabric over the toe. Begin sewing. Newer models of the felling foot have a slit where the needle enters, instead of the single hole of the older ones. This slit will allow you to insert lace, ribbon, rickrack or another embellishment as you sew the second line of stitches.

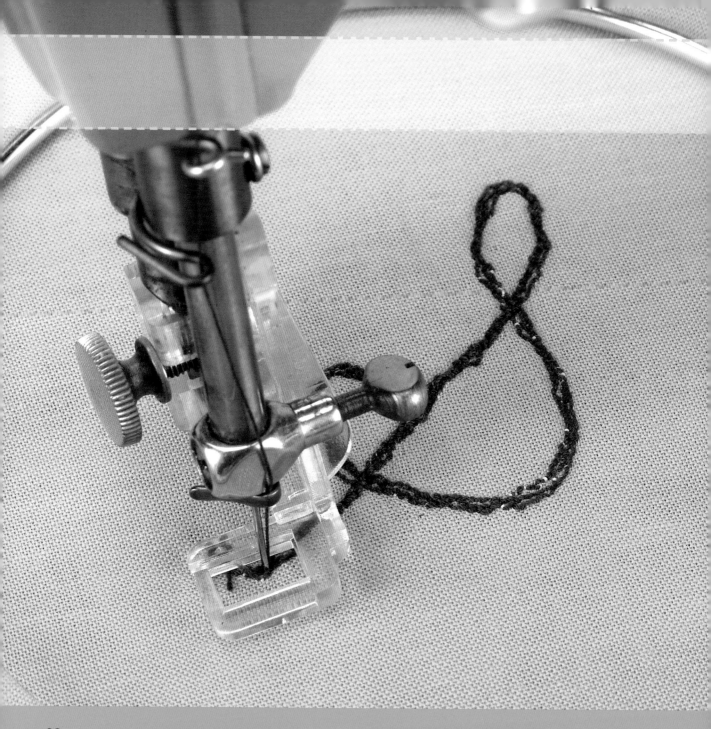

DARNING/EMBROIDERY/ FREE-MOTION QUILTING FOOT

This foot is specifically designed to barely touch the surface of your fabric, with very little pressure. Stitch placement is controlled by moving the fabric with your hands, not through the feed dogs.

There are a variety of darning, embroidery and quilting feet available. Regardless of which type you have, you must always use a feed cover plate or lower your machine's feed dogs. An embroidery hoop will keep your fabric taut as you sew.

Using the Darning/Embroidery/Free-Motion Quilting Foot

ATTACHING THE FOOT TO YOUR MACHINE

Remove your regular presser foot and attach the darning/embroidery/free-motion quilting foot to your presser bar. Place the feed cover plate on your machine. Be sure to use the darning plate specific to your sewing machine. When attaching, ensure the needle goes smoothly through the center of the hole in the darning plate. Ready your fabric in an embroidery hoop.

SIGNATURE STITCH

Create your initials or the letters of your name by using regular sewing thread in both the bobbin and the needle. You can embellish your script even more when using heavier thread or possibly silk thread. Tighten your tension a bit and, if necessary, possibly loosen the bobbin thread. Set your stitch length regulator at neutral (midway between forward and reverse).

TIP

When stitching, careful control of the embroidery hoop results in greater accuracy of your decorative stitch, or almost invisible mending. Try to match the speed of your sewing machine to the movement of your embroidery hoop, moving smoothly. You may find that moving the hoop away from you produces smoother embroidery stitching. To lock your stitching, take a few tacking stitches at the beginning and leave a tail of about 6" (15cm) at the end. Using your stiletto, push the tail to the underside of your fabric and hand tack.

ETCHING STITCH

Your thread choice and some simple adjustments may be all that is necessary to achieve various decorative stitches. An etching stitch is a free-motion embroidery stitch, usually following a design transferred onto your fabric. The use of an embroidery hoop is always recommended, and the feed dogs should be covered or dropped. Use a heavier thread in the bobbin and a fine thread in the needle. You may want to use a size 9 or 11 needle when using two- or three-cord embroidery thread. Always match your needle size to your top thread.

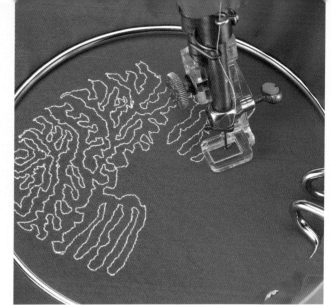

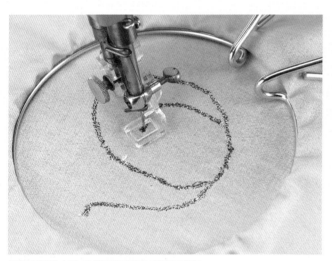

CIRCULAR OUTLINE STITCH

Outline a design with very small circles, or create double rows for more emphasis. Use regular sewing thread; however, you can achieve a more decorative stitch by using heavier thread in the needle or silk thread in the bobbin. Tighten the tension a bit and set the stitch length regulator at neutral. Move your hoop in very tiny circles, following your outline.

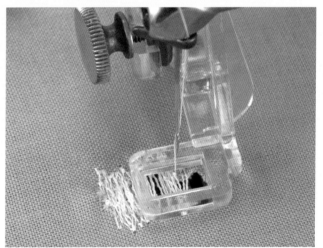

DARNING

Place your garment in an embroidery hoop, with the hole or tear in the center of the hoop. Begin stitching at one side, moving vertically across the hole. Continue with horizontal stitches from top to bottom. Match the grain of your fabric as closely as possible. Best results are achieved when the density and grain of your darning stitches match your fabric.

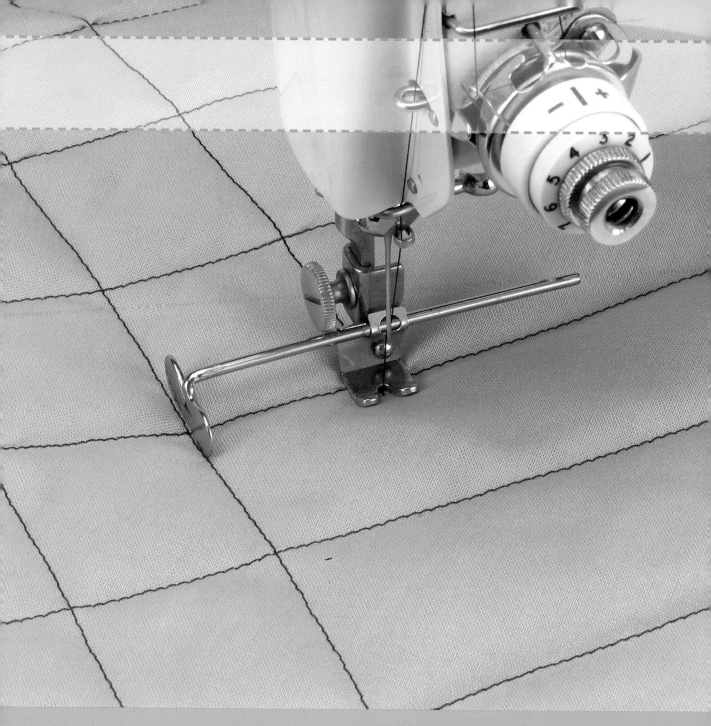

With the quilting foot you can embellish a quilt with squares, diamonds, blocks or rows and maintain consistent stitching and even spacing. You can also remove the guide bar for flowing patterns and free-motion stippling.

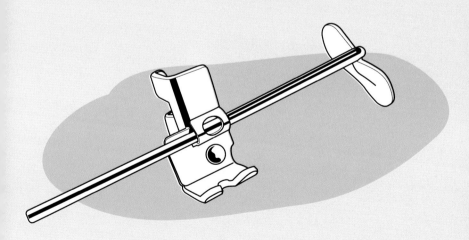

The quilting foot is a short, open foot with upturned toes and a detachable space guide. This design allows thick layers of fabric to fit easily under the needle without shifting or tight stitches. The open foot allows easy movement around curves, so quilting a pattern such as a vine or scroll is certainly an option and easy to achieve.

Although called a quilting foot, it is not used merely for quilting. Use this foot and the space guide any time you wish to sew multiple rows of decorative stitching. In addition, this foot is used in conjunction with the underbraider (see page 124) when sewing braids on your fabric.

Using the Quilting Foot

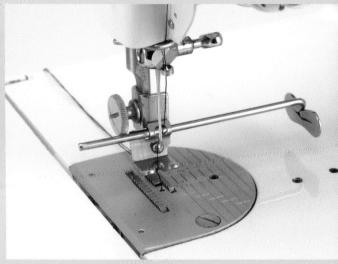

ATTACHING THE FOOT TO YOUR MACHINE

Replace your regular presser foot with the quilting foot. Adjust your stitch length as desired. Your quilting will have a more pleasing effect if the stitches are neither too long nor too short. Practice on a piece that has similar layers as your quilt until you find the stitch length you like.

ATTACHING AND USING THE SPACE GUIDE

The detachable space guide is inserted through a slot in the quilting foot. Place the guide to the right or left of your needle, adjusting the space width to match your quilting pattern. You can set your space guide to the right or left of the needle to better handle the bulk of your layered fabric. Some guides are designed to attach directly to the presser bar, between the quilting foot and the thumbscrew.

Sew your first line of stitching. For your second line of stitching, place the space guide over your first stitching. Continue sewing, each time placing the space guide on the previous row.

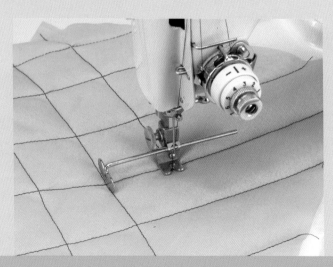

MAKING A DIAMOND PATTERN

Mark your fabric with a diagonal chalk line indicating your first line of stitching. Do this in both directions, sewing all of your stitching lines in one direction and then stitching in the other direction.

MAKING A ONE-OF-A-KIND JACKET

The quilting foot and space guide can be used to create a one-of-a-kind quilted jacket. You will create the quilt layer from your fabric, batting and backing. Cut out your pattern pieces, allowing several inches beyond the seam lines to allow for any shrinkage from your quilting. Quilt each piece. Reposition your pattern piece, cutting your seams accurately. Continue with your jacket construction as instructed. The quilting will add another dimension to your fabric and keep the layers together. You might follow a traditional quilting pattern, stippling or echo quilting around a motif in your fabric, or you might use contrasting thread color or embroidery floss.

MAKING A PUFFED, QUILTED HEM

Use your quilting foot and space guide to make a puffed, quilted hem for your bedspread. Cut a strip of quilt batting to the width you want for the completed hem. Turn back the hemline over the padding strip. Using your quilting foot and space guide, stitch three or four evenly spaced lines along the entire hem. The padding will puff out after stitching. You can, however, add additional batting for a puffier hem. Simply insert into your sewn strips.

TIP

Trapunto quilting gives a raised outline. Transfer your design to muslin. Baste to the wrong side of your fabric and stitch the lines, taking care not to stitch across any lines. Insert stuffing between the stitched lines and hand sew the opening closed.

Whether you have a vintage version or a newer reproduction, the walking foot, also known as an even feed foot, is designed to prevent slippage when stitching hard-to-sew fabrics such as velvet, leather and knits. It also helps to keep fabric layers from creeping while you are matching plaids.

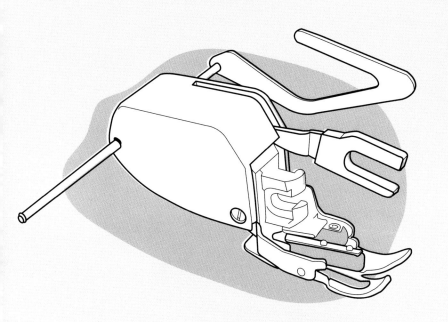

The walking foot is especially useful when stitching two different types of hard-to-sew fabrics together, such as satin binding on a blanket or lace on velveteen. This foot is perfect for your finished quilting or for top-stitching thick layers.

The purpose of the foot is to keep both fabrics together and prevent them from shifting under the needle. The walking foot has two toes: one moves in unison with the feed dogs, carrying the two layers of material and holding them firmly in place, while the second toe returns for the next stitch. Set your sewing machine to straight stitch with a center needle.

Using the Walking Foot

ATTACHING THE WALKING FOOT TO YOUR MACHINE

Remove the presser foot and fasten the walking foot to the presser bar, placing the lever onto your needle clamp. If you have a Singer walking foot, called a "penguin" due to its shape, attach it with the lever below the needle clamp instead of on it. You may have to remove your thread cutter if it prevents you from attaching the foot properly.

GUIDE ATTACHMENT

There are many variations of the walking foot. Not all of them are designed to accommodate a quilting guide. The guide is inserted through a hole in the back of the foot.

WORKING WITH FABRICS THAT SHIFT EASILY

When stitching satin binding to a blanket, pin the binding over the blanket and stitch approximately ¼" (6mm) from the top edge of the binding. You can add a second stitching close to the edge of the binding for additional decoration. If your fabric still tends to shift, cover the top layer with a sheet of tissue paper before stitching. You can easily tear it away after sewing.

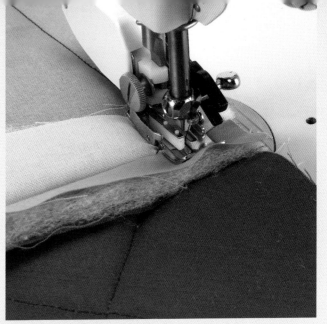

SEWING LAPPED SEAMS

The walking foot works perfectly for sewing lapped seams, which are appropriate for bulky fabrics, leather, fleece and nonfraying materials. Mark your seam lines and trim the upper material's seam allowance to the seam line. Place both pieces right sides up and overlap the upper and lower pieces, keeping the raw edge of the upper material aligned with the marked seam allowance of the lower material. Use a fabric adhesive to temporarily baste. Topstitch the upper material as close to the raw edge as possible and add a second stitching about ¼" (6mm) from the first.

MAKING A RAG QUILT

The walking foot can be used from start to finish when making a rag quilt with its multiple layers of fabric and batting. A rag quilt is composed of blocks sewn together in patchwork fashion, then washed and purposely frayed. Fabrics such as denim, flannel or broadcloth result in perfectly frayed edges. The batting can be traditional or flannel. All materials are cut into uniform squares, quilted and sewn together with a 1" (25mm) seam allowance. Seams are cut and the quilt tossed into the washer for the final fraying effect.

TIP

Use the walking foot for topstitching through multiple layers when constructing a jacket with facing, interfacing and garment materials. You can also use it when hemming an oilcloth tablecloth or to provide stability when stay-stitching knit fabrics around necklines.

If you sew yards and yards of sequins, lace, rickrack or other decorative trimming onto your sewing projects, this is a fashion foot worth learning to use. The hardest part is choosing your decorative notions!

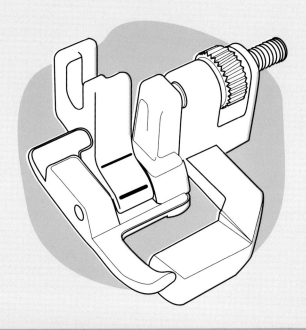

The sequin foot is designed with a small slot in the front, directly aligned with your needle to ensure that your trimming will be caught in each stitch. The slot can sew continuous strips of sequins, ribbons, rickrack or elastic up to ⅜" (9mm) wide. The foot works with either straight or zigzag stitching, with your needle set for center.

Using the Sequin Foot

ATTACHING THE SEQUIN FOOT TO YOUR MACHINE

Remove your presser foot and attach the sequin foot. The sequin foot has an adjusting screw to the right of the foot that allows you to adjust exactly where your stitch will fall. When sewing sequins, adjust it to fall in the center of each one; when sewing binding to your garment, adjust your first stitching line to fall on one edge, and then adjust it to sew your second stitching on the other edge.

SEWING SEQUINS

Slide your trimming through the slot in the front. Use a stiletto or thin screwdriver to help guide the trimming until you have at least 2" (5cm) on the back side of your needle. Place your fabric underneath the foot, lower the presser bar and begin sewing. As you sew, make sure the strand is feeding through easily. When sewing sequins, avoid twisting the strand to ensure that each one feeds into the slot running the same direction.

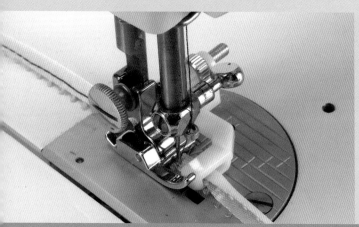

MAKING A THIN LOOP FOR USE AS A BUTTON LOOP

Insert prefolded binding, folded ribbon or lace into the slot of the foot. Adjust your stitching line to sew the outer edge. To add a second topstitch, put the binding back into the sequin foot and adjust the screw for your second line of stitching.

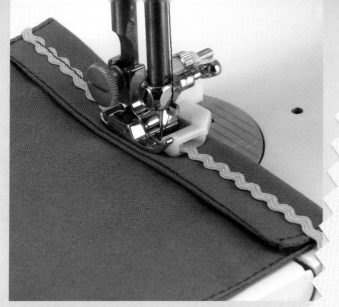

ADDING RICKRACK

Use the sequin foot when sewing your favorite apron pattern. Add small rickrack to your hem and pockets. For a festive look, use contrasting colors.

TIPS

When sewing with a sequin strip or other trimming that easily frays, put a small piece of tape around each end to prevent raveling. A sequin strip is held together by stitches, and once it is cut, the sequins can begin to fall out one by one.

You can easily add colorful rickrack to the ruffle of a child's dress or sew on thin elastic to gently gather your blouse cuffs. Use the sequin foot to sew a decorative pattern with soutache braid on the front of a blouse or on collars.

MAKING A RIBBON SKIRT

Make a ribbon skirt by using the sequin foot to add the ribbon to your fabric before cutting and sewing your favorite skirt pattern. Insert your ribbon into the slot, adjust for a center stitch, put your base fabric squarely under the foot and sew. Continue covering your base fabric in the design and coverage you wish. An A-line skirt pattern cut on the bias from fabric covered with rows and rows of ribbon creates an interesting effect. Be sure to match the ribbon rows at the seams.

Most buttonholers use templates to ensure that each buttonhole is perfect in size and shape. Others are called "complete buttonholers" because the size of the buttonhole is controlled by adjusting various levers.

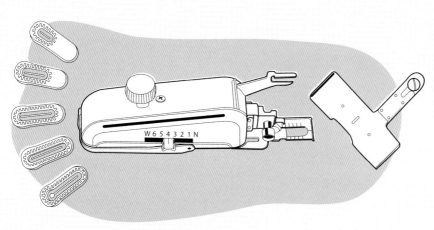

There are many types and brands of buttonholers. Your buttonholer should come with templates, an attaching screw, a feed cover plate and an instruction manual. Templates normally come in sizes 5/16" (8mm), 3/8" (9mm), 1/2" (13mm), 5/8" (16mm), 13/16" (20mm), and 1 1/16" (27mm) for straight buttonholes, and 5/8" (16mm) and 1 1/16" (27mm) for a keyhole buttonhole. Choose the template to match your button size. The feed cover plate that comes with your buttonholer must be used at all times to cover your feed dogs. Your manual will provide specifics for your own machine.

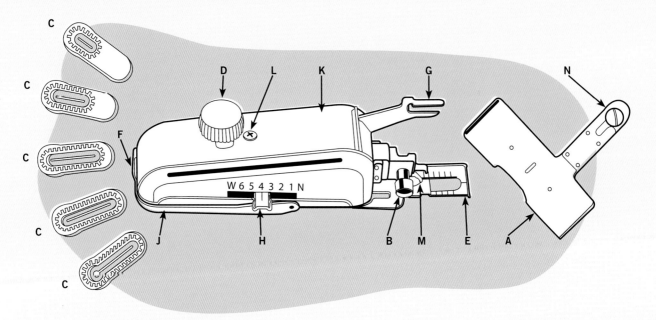

PARTS OF THE BUTTONHOLER

Your buttonholer parts may have different names, but all work in
basically the same manner.

A Feed Cover Plate: protects the feed dogs

B Slotted Clamping Screw: fastens to the presser bar

C Templates: control sizes and shapes of buttonholes

D Adjusting Knob: regulates the cloth clamp

E Cloth Clamp: grips the material

F Lock: locks the template retainer plate in position

G Form Arm: straddles the needle clamp

H Bight Adjuster: determines the width of the side stitch

J Template Retainer Plate: keeps templates in place

K Cover: encloses the moving parts

L Cover Screw: holds cover in place

M Stripper Foot: holds the fabric firmly

N Feed Cover Plate Screw: fastens the feed cover plate to
the machine

TIP

Some buttonholers are specific to a zigzag machine but can still be
used with a straight-stitcher. When using a buttonholer on a zigzag
sewing machine, the needle must always be in the center position.

Using a Buttonholer

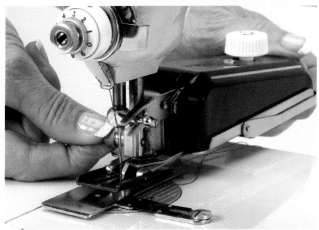

INSERTING A TEMPLATE IN YOUR BUTTONHOLER

A template must be inserted before placing the buttonholer on your machine. Measure your button to determine which template you should use. Turn the adjusting knob clockwise, and then turn the buttonholer over and unlock the retainer plate by pressing on the hinged edge, pushing it away from you. Open the template retainer plate and insert your template. You may need to turn the adjusting knob clockwise until the gears match and your template drops in. Close the retainer plate.

ATTACHING THE BUTTONHOLER TO YOUR MACHINE

Guide the attachment into position from the rear of the machine so the fork arm straddles the hub of the needle clamp, and fasten securely with the screw. You may need to turn or remove your thread cutter.

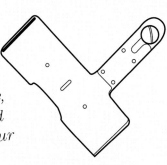

TIP

Before attaching the buttonholer to your machine, place the feed cover plate on the machine bed and fasten it with the thumbscrew. Check to be sure your needle passes through the center of the hole.

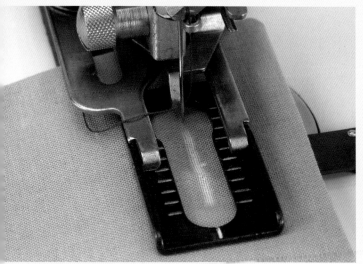

1

The buttonhole stitch width is determined by the bight adjuster. There are six settings that allow for the correct cutting space. To regulate, press the adjuster lever down and move it to your setting. Move it backward for wider stitches, and forward for narrower stitches. Remember, this is your cutting area.

Mark your buttonhole position. Turn the adjusting knob clockwise until the cloth clamp is all the way forward toward you and the needle appears at the center line on the back of the cloth clamp. Place your material under the cloth clamp and position your buttonhole in the center of the cloth clamp with the needle directly above the outer marking. Don't lower your needle yet.

2

Lower the presser bar. Turn the adjusting knob clockwise once again, moving the cloth clamp away from you. Stop when the cloth clamp is in position to sew up the right half of the buttonhole (as you are looking toward it). Take a stitch to draw the bobbin thread up and, holding both threads, take several stitches and ensure that they are out of the way of your buttonhole as you sew. Trim the loose threads as close to the fabric as possible. Stitch around your buttonhole twice for a raised effect.

TIP

When you are working buttonholes on very sheer materials, use a lightweight stabilizer that you can tear away when the buttonhole is completed. When working with velveteen, place water-soluble stabilizer between your fabric and the buttonholer. This will prevent the nap from hiding your buttonhole, and the stabilizer is easily washed out. If using velvet, lightly moisten a piece of cotton and dab your fabric until the stabilizer is gone.

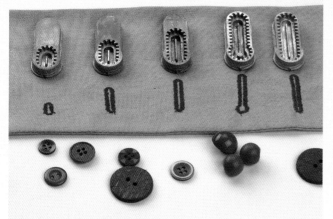

VARIOUS TEMPLATES AND THEIR RESULTS

Make a practice strip using each of your templates. By varying the stitch width and thread colors in your buttonholer, and by choosing the right buttons, you certainly can add that finished, professional look to your garments. Try sewing a double collar and adding a buttonhole and a huge Bakelite button.

"HANDWORKED" BUTTONHOLES

To create buttonholes that resemble handwork, set the bight adjuster to the widest setting. Stitch around twice. Without moving the material, change the bight adjuster to narrow and stitch around the buttonhole again. A contrasting thread can be used for the narrow stitch. The photo shows one half with the wide stitch only; the other has been sewn with both the wide and narrow. Practice with varying bight adjustments and thread colors to achieve the effect you want.

NOT JUST FOR BUTTONS

Sew two or three buttonholes at the top of a pocket. Run ribbon through the buttonholes. You might try an eyelet template if you have one.

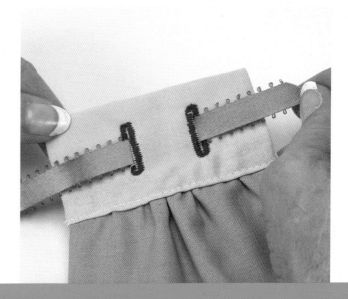

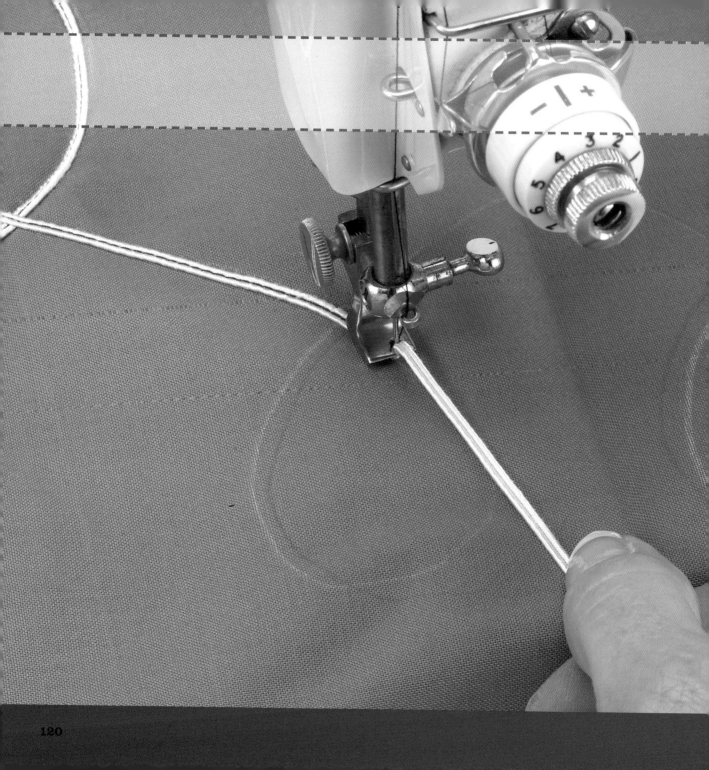

The braiding presser foot is especially suited to outlining with silk twist, wool yarn or soutache braid. The finished look will resemble hand embroidery or passementerie (see page 122). The foot works equally well using narrow ribbon to add a decorative trim to your project.

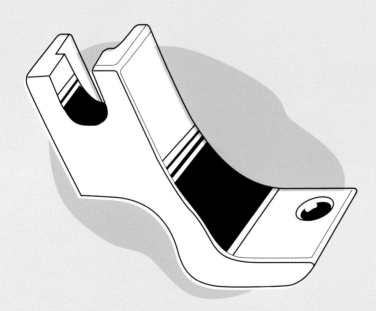

Braiding presser feet can be found in ¹⁄₁₆" (2mm), ¹⁄₃" (3mm) and ³⁄₁₆" (5mm) widths and in models for low, slant and snap-on shank sewing machines. Although you will most often use your braiding foot alone, it can be used with your underbraider (see page 124).

Using the Braiding Presser Foot

 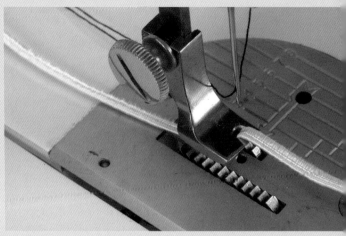

ATTACHING THE BRAIDING PRESSER FOOT TO YOUR MACHINE

The braiding presser foot is fastened to the presser bar in the same manner as the regular presser foot.

INSERTING YOUR TRIM

Insert the twist, yarn or ribbon through the small eyelet in front of the needle hole and pull it back under the braiding foot at least 2 to 3 inches (5cm to 8cm). While sewing, the trim is directly under the needle at all times, with the braiding foot holding it securely to your fabric. You can sew the thinnest trim and catch it with stitches every time.

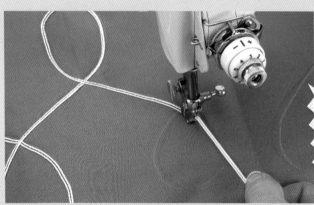

DEALING WITH PASSEMENTERIE

For passementerie, you'll need to place an appropriate design guide on your fabric. Designs that spiral or scroll and that are continuous work best. You can transfer your design directly onto your fabric with a removable marking pencil or use a design template basted to the top.

TERM TO KNOW

Passementerie *is the art of making decorative and often elaborate trimmings of braid, metallic cord, silk or beads. These are applied directly on the surface of clothing or home furnishings. Examples include military braid and the trims often seen on draperies and wedding gowns. The origin of bobbin lace is passementerie worked in white linen thread.*

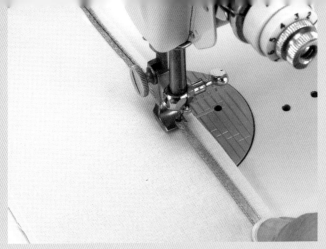

EDGING YOUR COLLAR WITH RIBBON

Insert your ⅛" (3mm) ribbon through the eyelet and pull back until you have about 2" (5cm) behind the needle. Lower the braiding presser foot and begin sewing, following the continuous lines of your pattern.

ADDING ELASTIC AND GATHERING AT THE SAME TIME

After marking the placement of your elastic, feed the elastic through the hole and beyond your needle. Take a few stitches to secure your elastic and begin sewing, stretching the elastic in front of the foot as necessary.

TIPS

When using a trim that frays easily, plan your design to begin and end within a seam. Thinner trimmings, such as wool yarn, can be brought to the underside of your fabric and hand tacked. When outlining with wool yarn or silk twist, the beginning and ending threads are drawn through to the underside of your material. Pull back over your braiding pattern and add a few stitches to hold the end in place.

You may need to stabilize your fabric before adding the trimming. Use lightweight interfacing, water-soluble interfacing or a combination of both placed underneath your material, in as many layers as necessary to prevent the trim from puckering.

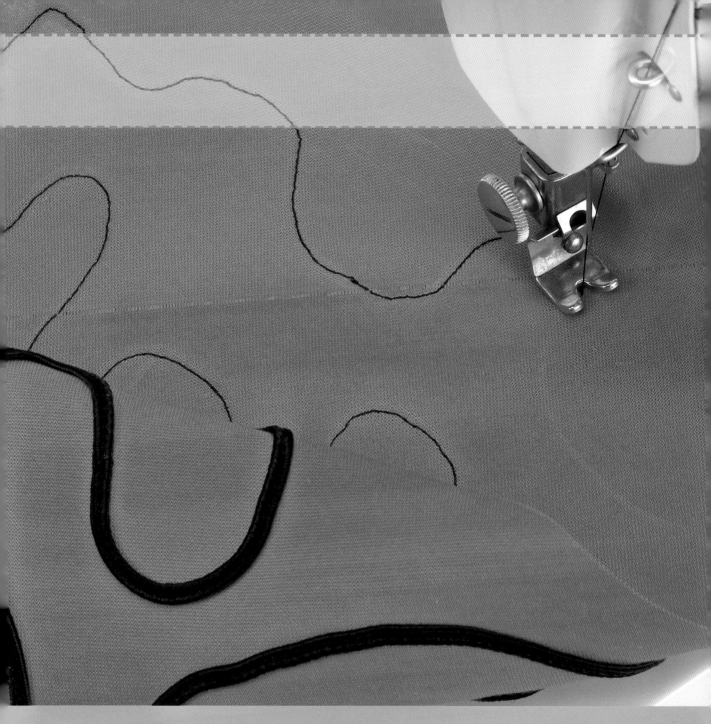

The underbraider is another attachment you can use for outlining a design or for attaching braid to your garment. Unlike the braiding presser foot, the underbraider follows the design on the wrong side of your material.

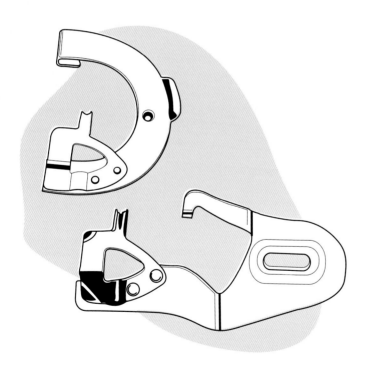

Each sewing machine has an underbraider that is specific to that machine model, because it must fit properly within the needle plate. The quilting foot usually is used in conjunction with the underbraider. The quilting foot has a short, wide opening that allows you to follow your pattern and also allows the braid to cross over with the proper tension and freedom of movement. A braiding presser foot may be used with the underbraider instead of the quilting foot.

Using the Underbraider

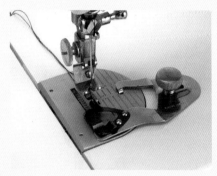

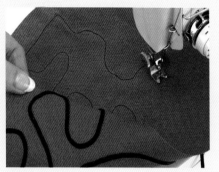

1

Attach the quilting foot to the machine and tighten it securely (see page 104). Attach the underbraider to the machine by pulling the needle slide plate outward to allow sufficient room for the prongs of the under-braider to fit under the machine's throat plate.

Most of your braiding designs will not require the quilting space guide, so you should remove it from the foot. However, any time you apply braid in straight rows, the guide can remain on to serve as a sewing guide.

2

To prepare your braid for sewing, slightly raise the underbraider's blue spring and insert the braid under the spring. It may be necessary to guide the braid under the spring by lifting the spring with a stiletto or screw-driver while simultaneously pulling the braid through. Pull through until you have at least 2" (5cm) beyond the needle. Check to ensure that the needle stitching falls in the center of the braid. If it doesn't, gently nudge the end of the braider tube in the proper direction.

3

The design you choose must be applied to the wrong side of the garment. Transfer your design to the wrong side of the fabric with a water-soluble marking pencil, or baste the pattern to the fabric. Place the fabric under the foot with the wrong side facing up. While you are following the design on the wrong side of your material, the braid will be applied to the right side. As you are sewing, simply guide the braid to ensure it does not twist before it enters the braider tube. Be sure the braid can flow freely from the roll.

 TIPS

Any braid that fits in the underbraider tube and allows the needle to stitch through its center may be used. In the past, popular braids were cotton or silk soutache and pigtail braid. Soutache braid is available in many sewing shops in a wide array of colors.

A continuous scrolling and looping design works best. If possible, begin and end at a seam. If not, you can securely fasten and hide the ends by making a small hole next to the braid with your stiletto, pulling the ends through to the underside of the fabric, and hand sewing in place with a few stitches.

SEWING STRAIGHT, EVENLY SPACED BRAIDS

Using the quilting space guide along with the quilting foot ensures straight, evenly spaced braids (see page 104 for instructions).

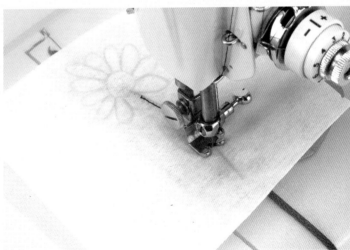

COPYING A DESIGN THAT REPEATS WITHIN YOUR PROJECT

Copy the design onto numerous stacked sheets of pellon or thin paper using your sewing machine. Attach the quilting foot to your machine and, without threading, follow the design. This will perforate the paper, giving you multiple copies. Pin the paper to the fabric to be embellished, and when you have finished sewing, tear the paper away. You also can make photocopies of your design; just ensure that they are all the same size.

WORKING WITH DELICATE MATERIALS

When adding braid to soft fabrics, organza or tulle, a few simple steps will ensure proper stitching. Put your design on paper and pin it to the material. If the fabric is still difficult to sew, a piece of thin paper can be placed underneath the foot.

If you are using this foot for quilting, your stitch will be very close to the seam, allowing your finished quilting to be very subtle. When you use this foot to stitch in the ditch along neck or armhole facing, the stitching virtually disappears because it is directly in the seam line. Use a matching or invisible thread for the best results.

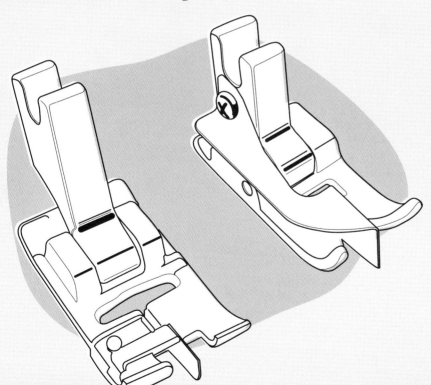

The stitch-in-the-ditch foot is also called an edge-joining foot. Against the right toe is a metal guide that allows you to accurately follow your seam line. Use this foot to stitch in the ditch, join lace to fabric, topstitch or attach lace to lace.

Using the Stitch-in-the-Ditch Foot

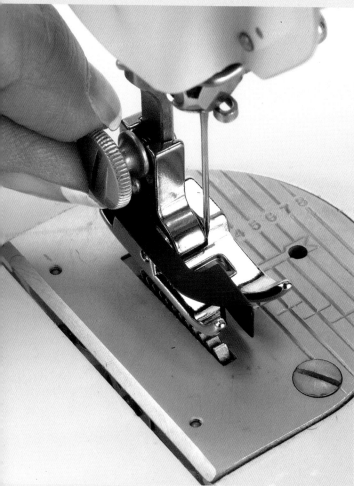

ATTACHING THE STITCH-IN-THE-DITCH FOOT TO YOUR MACHINE

Remove your regular presser foot and replace it with the stitch-in-the-ditch foot, tightening it securely. Regulate your pressure bar according to the bulk of your fabric. Adjust your tension according to your thread choice.

LET THE BAR BE YOUR GUIDE

Straight, accurate stitch-in-the-ditch quilting depends upon early preparation and initially straight, even seams. Because the foot is following the seam line, if it is uneven, then your final quilting also will be uneven. When piecing your quilt, use this foot to guide your seam allowance for a perfect ⅛" (3mm) margin.

PRESSING IMPORTANCE

Pressing is equally important. Press to one side, which allows the sewing foot to stitch on the "lower" seam—in the ditch. This side of your seam has less bulk, especially when stitching over multiple seams. This will create a nice ⅛" (3mm) quilting seam that is straight and even.

CREATING HEIRLOOM FABRIC

Use Swiss embroidered edging between two pieces of lace. For a vintage look, try embroidered fabric inserts between your lace and other embroidery, creating your own heirloom-quality fabric to work with.

SEWING LACE TO THE EDGE OF A TUCK

Fold and press the tuck. Place your lace over the fold, matching the lace edge to the fold. Place the piece under the foot, aligning the metal guide where you want your stitch line. Open and press the tuck and lace to one side. Continue with additional lace and tucks.

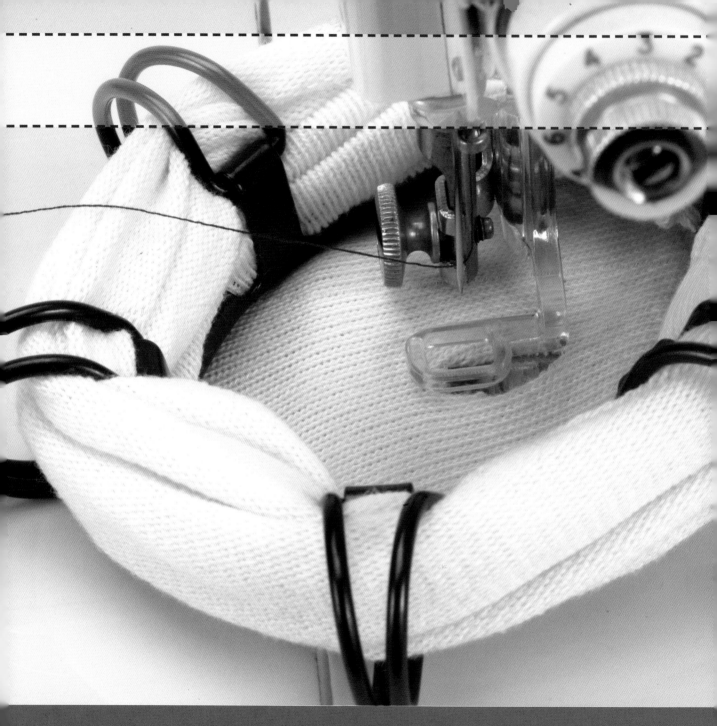

In previous generations, it was quite necessary for every garment and pair of stockings to last as long as possible. This accessory for the sewing machine provided a quicker, easier method of darning.

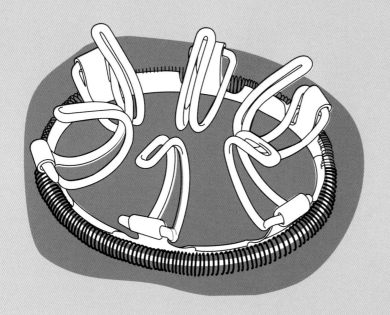

A darner can be used to mend a variety of items, such as sweaters, shirt sleeves, stockings, socks, dresses and pants. There are two sizes of darners: a smaller stocking darner and a larger darner for heavier items. Your darner should have a spiral spring in good condition and a frame with six arms.

Using the Stocking Darner

TIP

Best results are achieved when using a feed cover plate to cover your feed dogs. A cover plate is not supplied with the stocking darner; however, you can use any that fits your machine. You also should use a darning/ embroidery foot; this prevents the fabric from rising with each needle stitch. There are many types to choose from (see page 99).

1

Remove the spring from the frame and push the six arms toward the inside of the frame.

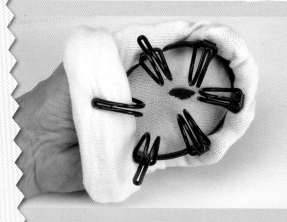

2

Place your hand inside the sock and the darner over it, with the hole at the center. Using the hand that's inside the sock, grasp hold of the frame and turn the sock inside out. Place the spring back on, fitting it into the grooves.

3

Beginning at the top and continuing to the darner frame, begin rolling the sock. Fold the six arms over the stocking to hold it in place while darning.

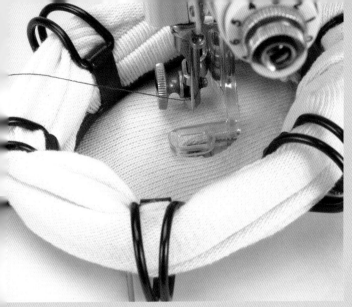

4

Replace your regular presser foot with a darning foot (see page 100 for instructions).

5

Place the darner under the darning foot. Begin by sewing back and forth, and then up and down, continuing the pattern until the hole has been completely darned. Follow the weave or the knit pattern of the fabric as closely as possible. This will create new material that is quite strong and durable.

TIP

When using a darner to repair holes in clothing or linens:

Place the hole in the center of the darner, so the stitching will be on the right side of your garment.

Begin rolling your fabric until the excess is away from your sewing. Place the six arms over the rolled garment. Put the spiral spring on, ensuring that it fits into the grooves.

Place the darner under your darning foot and begin to sew as previously instructed.

The zigzagger gives you the ability to add a variety of decorative stitches using your straight-stitch sewing machine.

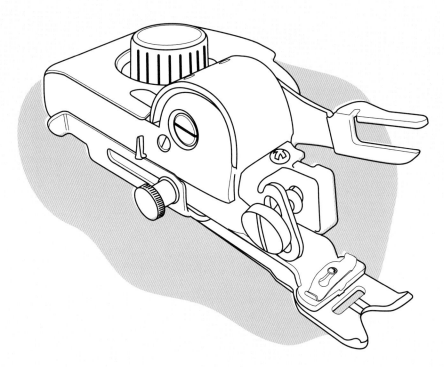

Stitch patterns are achieved through cams, each one giving you a choice of ornamental stitching such as zigzag, arrowhead, blind stitch, domino and scallop stitches. The zigzag pattern creates a uniform stitch useful for tucking, appliqué and seam finishes. You might use the blind stitch pattern for edging seams or making tucks. Combine several patterns for a decorative edge on children's clothing.

Using the Zigzagger

ATTACHING THE ZIGZAGGER TO YOUR MACHINE

Remove the regular presser foot and raise the presser bar. Guide the zigzagger attachment into position from the rear, so the fork straddles the hub of the needle clamp. Tighten securely.

ADDING A DECORATIVE CAM TO THE ZIGZAGGER

Raise the presser bar. Lift and swing up the top cover. Lift out the zigzag cam and insert another. Close the cover, lower the presser foot and begin sewing.

TIP

Each cam's design can be altered by changing the bight and stitch settings. Because each cam is easily removed from the top of the zigzagger, combinations of designs can be achieved by beginning with one stitch pattern and then continuing with another. The zigzagger is also designed so you can lift the lever behind the fork arm and return to straight stitching.

LOOKING BACK

Adjustable zigzaggers were once made without cams; stitching patterns were changed by moving a stitch regulator on the side of the attachment.

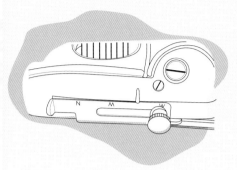

A sliding bar on the side of the zigzagger controls the bight; moving it forward and backward changes the width of the pattern. Additional changes may be made by adjusting your machine's stitch length.

With the bight at 0 and a short stitch length, your zigzag pattern will be narrow and close together.

By moving the bight and increasing the stitch length, the zigzag stitch increases somewhat in width and is considerably lengthened.

TIP

When sewing on sheer or lightweight fabrics, a lightweight tear-away stabilizer placed underneath the attachment foot will produce the best stitch.

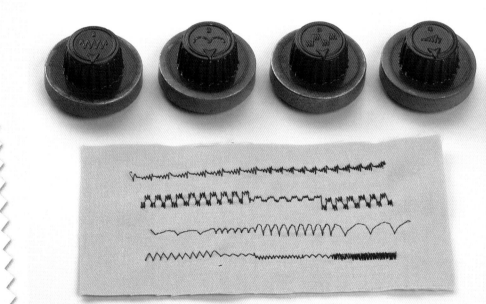

In addition to the zigzag stitch, additional cams can produce decorative stitches like the arrowhead, domino and scallop.

ADDING CORDING OR HEAVY THREAD

Place the fabric under the foot and insert the end of the cord between the toes of the zigzagger and beyond the needle several inches (centimeters). Use two or more cords for a different effect.

SEWING LACE TO FABRIC

Insert lace between two pieces of fabric to create a vintage effect or for open lace appliqué. Place your lace on top of your fabric, the right sides of your fabric facing up, with the fabric extending beyond the lace about ⅛" (3mm). Place underneath the center of your zigzagger. Adjust your zigzag stitch length so one stitch falls on the fabric/lace layer and the other falls onto the lace. As your skill increases, you can decrease the amount of fabric under your lace, eventually sewing with the lace and the fabric butted against each other.

ATTACHING LACE TO LACE

To attach lace to lace, align your lace so edges are butted together. Adjust your zigzag stitch so that one stitch catches the right lace and the next catches the left. If your machine is straight-stitch only and you do not have a zigzagger attachment, you can achieve a similar effect by overlapping your lace in the center so the presser foot falls on the edge of each. Sew slowly, keeping the lace overlapped and the stitches in the center.

Resources

Machine Manuals

All sewing machine companies realize that machine manuals get lost and are happy to assist you in replacing an original manual for any sewing machine. Whether you found one at an estate sale or yard sale, or inherited your mother's, try the machine's manufacturer first. Before contacting the company, determine your machine's make and model. Most replacement manuals usually cost between fifteen and twenty-five dollars.

MANUFACTURERS

BABY LOCK
www.babylock.com

BERNINA INTERNATIONAL AG
www.berninausa.com

BROTHER INTERNATIONAL CORP.
www.brother-usa.com
/homesewing

ELNA INTERNATIONAL
www.elnausa.com

HUSQVARNA VIKING
www.husqvarnaviking.com

JANOME
www.janome.com

KENMORE (SEARS)
www.sears.com

PFAFF
www.pfaff.com/global

RICCAR AMERICA, INC.
www.riccar.com/products
/sewing-machines

SINGER SEWING COMPANY
www.singerco.com
/accessories/manuals.html

WHITE SEWING MACHINE CO.
www.whitesewing.com

OTHER SOURCES

ISMACS INTERNATIONAL (INTERNATIONAL SEWING MACHINE COLLECTORS' SOCIETY)
www.ismacs.net/singer/manuals/index.html
This site is another valuable source of information for locating older manuals. Many are available as PDF files.

Attachments, Patterns and Notions

There are many places to find the attachments mentioned in this book. Stop by your local sewing store or sewing machine repair shop to find these items. Or shop online at your favorite Internet retailer.

MANUFACTURERS

SINGER SEWING COMPANY
www.singerco.com
Singer customer resource pages:
www.singerco.com/resources

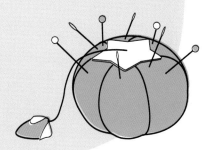

Index

A

Adjustable hemmer, 71–73
Adjustable tape-stitching presser
    foot, 49–51
Adjustable zipper/cording foot, 87–89
Attachment foot, 29–31
Attachment holder, 30

B

Basting, 20
Bias cutting gauge, 37–39
Bias strips
    cutting, 38
    fabric yardage, 39
    gauge, 38
    piecing, 39
    prefolded, 39
Bias-tape maker, 45, 46
Binder, 37, 39, 41–43
Binding, 37, 43
    fusible, 47
    lattice, 43
    two-tone, 43
Blind hemming, 13
Bobbins
    burrs, 17
    loading, 16, 17
    size, 18
Braiding presser foot, 121–123
Braids, 76, 126
Buttonholer, 115–119
Button loops, 51

C

Clamps, 24, 25
Cloth guide, 33–35
Complete buttonholers, 115
Cording, 37, 88, 89
    tubular, 92

D

Darning, 99, 101, 133–135
Double shirring foot, 83–85

E

Edge-joining foot, 129
Edge stitcher, 75–77
Elastic, 123
Embroidery, 99, 100
Embroidery hoop, 100
Etching stitch, 101
Even feed foot, 107

F

Fabrics
    delicate, 127
    fraying, 37, 95
    hard-to-sew, 107
    heirloom, 131
    stabilizers, 118, 123, 139
    weight, 20
Facings, 37
Feed cover plate, 117, 134
Felled seam, 63, 65, 95–97
Felling foot, 95–97
Foot hemmer, 63–65

Free-motion quilting foot, 99
French seams, 43, 77
Fusible-tape maker, 45, 47

G

Gathering foot, 79–81
Gathers, 57, 59
Graybar Manufacturing Company, 9
Griest (Greist), John, 8
Griest Manufacturing Company, 8

H

Hemmers, 29, 30, 63–65
    adjustable, 71–73
    set, 67–69
Hemming, 69
    adding ruffle, 77
    creasing, 68

L

Lace
    adding while hemming, 65
    to fabric, 140
    to lace, 76, 140

N

Needles, double, 85

P

Passenmenterie, 122
Pigtail braids, 126
Pillow seam, 93
Pin tucks, 55

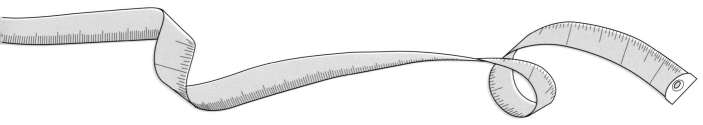

Piping, 77, 88
Pleating, 57, 61
Pressure regulator, 20, 22
Problems. see troubleshooting
Projects, 15
Puckering, 22, 93
Puffing, 81

Q
Quilting, 99
Quilting foot, 103–105
Quilting guide, 80

R
Rag quilt, 109
Rickrack, 51, 113
Ruffler, 57–61
Ruffles, 43, 60, 61

S
Scissors cutting gauge, 38
Seam allowance, 33, 96
Seam guide, 33–35
Seams
        curved, 19, 35, 42, 93
        elasticity, 19
        felled, 95
        lapped, 109
        visible lines, 97
Sequin foot, 111–113
Sequins, 112, 113
Sewing machine
        automatic, 13

choosing, 15–18
computerized, 14
electronic, 13
features, 16
mechanical, 13
portable, 15
semiautomatic, 13
sergers, 14
set-up, 19
shopping for, 16, 18
used, 17
Shank type, 23
Shirring, 80, 83, 84, 85
Signature stitch, 100
Singer Manufacturing Company, 8, 11
Smocking, 81
Soutache braids, 126
Stitches, uneven, 22
Stitch-in-the-ditch foot, 129–131
Stitch length, 19, 20, 79
Stitch regulator, 19
Stocking darner, 133–135
Straight-stitch machines, 13, 116

T
Tape-stitching presser foot, 49–51
Tension, 21
Thread
        breaking, 18
        loose, 18
        snarled, 51
        tension, 21
Topstitching, 20, 109

Trapunto quilting, 105
Trim, decorative, 111, 122, 123. see
        also passenmenterie
Troubleshooting, 18, 22
Tucker, 53–55
Tucks, 53

U
Underbraider, 125–127

W
Waffle shirring, 85
Walking foot, 107–109
Welting foot, 88, 91–93
Western Electric, 9
Willcox & Gibbs, 10

Z
Zigzagger, 137–139
Zigzag stitch, 13
Zippers, 89

Sew many more ideas!

101 WAYS TO USE YOUR FIRST SEWING MACHINE

Elizabeth Dubicki

This fresh and contemporary approach to an age-old tradition gives readers instruction and inspiration to be successful using a basic sewing machine. This handy guide is perfect to take along when buying fabric and supplies, and features a lay-flat format for hands-free use. Step-by-step instructions let you achieve inexpensive custom looks for the home and wardrobe tips and tricks to help sewers expand their skills and use of their machine.

ISBN 13: 978-0-89689-309-2
ISBN 10: 0-89689-309-X
Hardcover w/ encase spiral, 192 pages, YFSM

SEW WITH CONFIDENCE

Nancy Zieman

Beginning or aspiring sewers will learn the skills they need and gain confidence in their work with this helpful guide! Sew With Confidence teaches basic sewing skills and then moves on to explain more complex techniques, encouraging readers to take their skills to the next level with more involved projects. The book includes information on materials and tools needed to get started, sewing and serger machines, organizing the sewing area, patterns, fabrics and more.

ISBN 13: 978-0-87349-811-1
ISBN 10: 0-87349-811-9
Paperback, 128 pages, SWWC

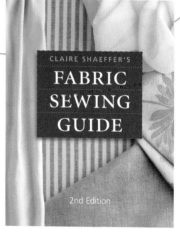

CLAIRE SHAEFFER'S FABRIC SEWING GUIDE, 2nd Edition

Claire Schaeffer

This new, full-color edition is the sewing enthusiasts' one-stop resource, with answers to the most common fabric sewing questions. In addition to an extensive glossary, this must-have guide includes a fabric and fiber dictionary, easy-to-read charts for needle sizes and thread, stabilizer types and much more.

ISBN 13: 978-0-89689-536-2
ISBN 10: 0-89689-536-X
Paperback, 504 pages, Z0933

Discover imagination, innovation and inspiration at
www.mycraftivity.com
CONNECT. CREATE. EXPLORE.